THE
CONTEMPLATIVE
LIFE

Other Writings of Joel S. Goldsmith

THE CONTEMPLATIVE LIFE

Joel S. Goldsmith

Edited By
Lorraine Sinkler

I-Level
Acropolis Books, Publisher
Lakewood, CO

THE CONTEMPLATIVE LIFE
First Acropolis Books Edition 1999
© 1963, 1991 by Joel Goldsmith

All Bible quotations are taken from THE KING JAMES VERSION

Published by Acropolis Books, Publisher, under its I-Level imprint, under an arrangement with Citadel Press, an imprint of Carol Publishing Group.
All rights reserved.

Printed in the United States of America.

No part of this book may be used or reproduced in any manner whatsoever without written permission except in the case of brief quotations embodied in critical articles and reviews.
For information contact:

Acropolis Books, Inc.
Lakewood, Colorado

http://www.acropolisbooks.com

Library of Congress Cataloging-in-Publication Data

Goldsmith, Joel S., 1892–1964.
    The contemplative life / Joel S. Goldsmith; edited by Lorraine Sinkler.
- - 1ˢᵗ Acropolis Books ed.
        p.   cm.
    Originally published: Secaucus, NJ: University Books, 1963.
    Includes bibliographical references.
    ISBN 1-889051-45-4 (hardcover : alk. paper)
    ISBN 1-889051-44-6 (paperback : alk. paper)
    1. Spiritual life.   I. Sinkler, Lorraine.   II. Title.
BP610.G641554 1994
299' .93--dc21   99-28539
                                                                      CIP

This book is printed on acid free paper that meets the American National Standards Institute Z 39.48 Standard

Except the Lord build the house,
they labour in vain that build it. . . .
—Psalm 127

"Illumination dissolves all material ties and binds
men together with the golden chains of spiritual
understanding; it acknowledges only the leadership of the Christ; it has no ritual or rule but the
divine, impersonal universal Love; no other
worship than the inner Flame that is ever lit at the
shrine of Spirit. This union is the free state of
spiritual brotherhood. The only restraint is the
discipline of Soul; therefore, we know liberty
without license; we are a united universe without
physical limits, a divine service to God without
ceremony or creed. The illumined walk without
fear—by Grace."

—*The Infinite Way* by Joel S. Goldsmith

TABLE OF CONTENTS

TABLE OF CONTENTS

TABLE OF CONTENTS

DAILY PREPARATION FOR SPIRITUAL LIVING

Students Must Never Advance Beyond the Principles–When Is a Spiritual Experience a Real Experience?–Evolving States of Consciousness–The Impersonal Source of All Discord–Daily Practice Is Essential–Never Believe That You Know What to Pray For–The Practice of the Principles Is an Aid to Meditation–Across the Desk

MEDITATION ON LIFE BY GRACE

God's Omnipresence–Why We Do Not Experience the Kingdom–God Is Your Dwelling Place–Dealing with Daily Problems–Only One Legitimate Desire–Your Own Will Come to You–Seek *Me*–Self-Surrender–Across the Desk

SUPPLY AND SECRECY

Gratitude as an Evidence of Receptivity–The Seed Must Be Nurtured in Secret–Practice but Do Not Preach–Across the Desk

THE SPIRITUAL CHRISTMAS

Isaiah Reveals the Christ–Receptivity to the Christ Is Greater in Time of Need–The Rejection of the Christ–The Christ Dissolves All Evil–The Impersonal Christ-Life

The
Contemplative
Life

~ 1 ~

Conscious Awareness

Many persons who are seeking for truth or striving to
find a way that will lead them out of the inharmonies
and discords of life gather the impression that there is
some quick or short way of overcoming all their problems; that there is some kind of a message that they can
read in books or hear from the lips of a teacher or
lecturer, that will quickly take them away from the
troubles of a material way of living into the harmonies of
the spiritual life. This is the mistake that is made in every
one of the Western countries.

It is not so in the East, where the relative unimpor-
tance of time is better understood and where it is realized that an evolution of consciousness can take place
only over a span of years. But in the West, where in one
short life-cycle we have gone from lamplight to modern
electric lighting and from the horse and buggy era to
automobiles and airplanes, where there has been an
increase in the speed of travel from 100 miles an hour to
thousands of miles, we do not seem to have sufficient
time or sufficient interest to take the time for the development of spiritual consciousness. Because of this
unbelievably rapid progress, materially and mechani-
cally, which has set the tempo of our times, many think
that it is possible to apply this same accelerated speed to
the spiritual life.

But when it comes to spiritual unfoldment and spiritual progress, it is quite a different story. There, an element of time enters into the situation, and it is this element of time that our Western world seems unwilling to accept, or may not be able or prepared to accept.

It is often possible for those of us who come to a spiritual teaching to have our problems quickly met—physical, mental, moral, or financial—but, of course, even if all our major problems were quickly met, we still would be no better off than we were before, except for a little temporary relief from the world's discords, because regardless of what freedom we attain through the help of a practitioner or a teacher, we still have to evolve in our own consciousness in order to maintain and sustain that freedom.

The Function of the Transcendental Consciousness

Although work such as that of the Infinite Way does help students to overcome their present physical, mental, moral, or financial difficulties, this is not its primary function. The goal of this particular Message is the spiritualization of consciousness which, in the Western world, is described as the attainment of that mind which was in Christ Jesus: Christ-consciousness or the transcendental consciousness. In the East, this same goal is called the attainment of Buddhahood, or the Buddha-mind, or Buddhi, but all those terms mean the same thing, because whether one receives enlightenment in the East or in the West, the result is precisely the same.

The point that I would like you to see at this moment is that the goal of all religious work should be spiritual enlightenment, that is, the attainment of spiritual light. When this light comes, it comes as a transcendental state of consciousness, and it is the attainment of this transcendental state of consciousness that really constitutes the activity of the Infinite Way, and is basic to its teaching.

The first question that would naturally arise in any seeker's mind is: What is the transcendental state of consciousness and what function does it perform in my experience? My answer to that is that the transcendental or spiritual consciousness is a state of consciousness which instantaneously releases an individual from all material concern. That, I believe, is its first and greatest function in our lives. It releases us from fear and doubt; it releases us from concern over what we shall eat, or what we shall drink, or wherewithal we shall be clothed. Most important of all, it releases us from the fear of death.

Whether we have ever consciously thought about it or not, all of us on the human plane of life fear death. In fact, the one reason we fear disease is because the natural consequence of disease is death. We also fear age because age carries with it the connotation of coming death. Death, because of its inevitability, is that which is feared, and the fear of death is often the very cause of our diseases.

With the first touch of spiritual light, however, all fear of death disappears, because that light reveals that there is no death and that the experience of passing from this plane of life to what is called the next is not really a death: it is just another experience like our birth; it is a passing from one phase of life to another. In other words, life never had a beginning; therefore our coming into this world was but a coming forth from another phase of life.

Some of those who have attained a certain degree of illumination are able to go back and see different aspects of their life prior to their present earth experience. Although that may not always be possible, nevertheless, with the first taste of spiritual light, we do realize that, since there is no death, there need be no fear of it, and once that fear is eliminated, the body seems to adjust itself, and health begins to manifest instead of disease and the signs of age.

The Transcendental Consciousness
Brings a Release from Concern for Persons or Things

Furthermore, when spiritual light has once touched the soul or consciousness of an individual, never again can there be concern about what we call supply: what we shall eat or drink, wherewithal we shall be clothed, or how much money we shall or shall not have. The reason for this lack of concern constitutes the sum and substance of what must be our goal if we are to attain the spiritual way of life.

In the ordinary human sense of life, concern is nearly always for things, persons, or conditions. If at this very moment we were to think about what it is that worries us most we would in all probability find that our fear is undoubtedly about something in the form of an effect: a person, a condition, a thing, an amount, a body, a bit of money, or a piece of property. Always it is about an effect, and what concerns us is always in the realm of an effect.

As human beings, are we not always striving for some thing, some person, or some condition? It may be for a living, for fame, or for wealth; it may be for an education;

it may be for health–but nearly always our life is centered on the attainment of something or other.

Most human beings fail during their lifetime to attain what they have been seeking and pass out of this life frustrated without ever having achieved their goals. Those who do reach their goals find that this achievement brings little permanent satisfaction. Some attain temporarily the perfect body, only later on to witness its disintegration; some attain the wealth that they have sought, and then after they have it, find that when they have eaten three times a day and have an ample wardrobe of clothing, all the rest of their money is of so little use that their efforts to attain it seem almost foolish in retrospect. Rarely does money ever give a person the satisfaction that he thought it would when he was struggling and striving for it. And I do not have to remind you that fame gives back even less of satisfaction and is even more of an empty bauble than is wealth.

This does not mean that there is anything wrong about the attainment of fame or wealth or health or a perfect body. On the contrary, all these are the added things that inevitably come when the spiritual way of life becomes our first and major concern. In the spiritual way of life, our first step is to disregard temporarily our concern for things, persons, and conditions, and center our attention on attaining a conscious realization of our Source.

Becoming One with Our Source

It is a part of the Christian teaching, as given in the fifteenth chapter of John, that when we are one with our Source, we bear fruit richly, but when we are separated from that Source, we are as a branch of a tree that is cut off and withereth. The Ninety-first Psalm also promises that none of the evils of this world will come nigh the dwelling place of those who have made God their dwelling place, again indicating to us that our oneness with our Source is what separates us from the evils of this world and maintains in our experience the harmonies of heaven.

The revelation was given to me that in my conscious oneness with God, in being consciously one with my Source, the good things of life were added unto me, that is, I was at-one with all good: with every form of good that might ever be necessary in my experience. The Master said, "Take no thought for your life, what ye shall eat, or what ye shall drink; nor yet for your body, what ye shall put on. . . . But seek ye first the kingdom of God, and his righteousness; and all these things shall be added unto you."[1] And so it was that this very same consciousness revealed to me that when I am consciously one with God, I am instantaneously one with all the good necessary for my experience. Therefore, I must stop taking thought about my supply, my health, or my home. I must stop taking anxious thought or concern for the things of this world, and I must make every effort to abide *consciously* in my oneness with God.

The vital part and the heart of that revelation is that we are *already* one with God. We are already one with our Lifestream, or the Source of our life. As a matter of fact, "I and my Father are one"[2] is a relationship that is indivisible and indestructible. It is an impossibility for my Father and me to become separate because we are not two: we are one! We are and always have been one with our Source, one with God.

The reason that the harmonies of heaven and the blessings of divine Grace do not come into our experience as they should lies in the one word *consciously.* Nothing can enter your life or mine except as it enters through our consciousness. This is the greatest law, the greatest discovery, unfoldment, or revelation that has ever come into my experience: *nothing can come into your or my experience except through our own consciousness.*

In other words, you consciously brought yourself to the reading of this book. There are millions of people not reading it and, therefore, not a spark of this message has entered their consciousness, so that they are not even aware that anything of this sort exists in the world, but even you who are reading these words could, if you so desired, shut out of your consciousness the message that is being brought to you. You could sit right where you are, completely unaware of the import of these words, reading them with your eyes only, and they would make no impression upon you; they would not enter the depths, the realm, of your consciousness. If you are to benefit by this message, there must be a responsive activity within your consciousness. Later, as you go deeper into the study of the Infinite Way, you will discover how you have admitted the inharmonies and the discords of life into your experience through your own consciousness and how you can eliminate them after they are there or how you can prevent their taking root there, because nothing can transpire in your experience except as an activity of your own consciousness.

Although you and I are one with God, although we are one with our Source, one with the Fount of everlasting life, one with the Source of infinite abundance, these can come into our experience only through our acceptance of them in our own consciousness. In other words, when we begin to declare within ourselves that there is a Source of life, then it must be true that that Source forever governs Its* creation and forever maintains and sustains that which It has brought forth into expression.

And so from the moment that we consciously perceive that we are always in the bosom of our Father and always one with our Source, indivisible and inseparable from that Source, it becomes clear to us that all that is flowing forth from that Lifestream, all that emanates from that infinite Source, is pouring Itself into, through, and from our individual consciousness.

Gaining the Consciousness of the Presence

As we abide in this, that is, *if* we abide in this Word, if we let this Word abide in us, we shall bear fruit richly. The secret of the spiritual life is to recognize consciously—consciously realize, accept, and declare—our oneness with our infinite, immortal, eternal Source, and accept the scriptural statement that all that the Father has is ours and that the place whereon we stand is holy ground. Not only must we accept it, but we must abide in it every single day of the week, bringing to conscious remembrance the truth:

---

*In the spiritual literature of the world, the varying concepts of God are indicated by the use of such words as "Father," "Mother," "Soul," "Spirit," "Principle," "Love," or "Life." Therefore, in this book the author has used the pronouns "He" and "It," or "Himself" and "Itself," interchangeably in referring to God.

"I and my Father are one."[3] *I am one with my Source, and all that is flowing forth from God is flowing into my experience.**

When we perceive that this is true and are willing to make it a part of our *conscious* experience, we are engaging in a form of contemplative meditation. This contemplative meditation, which should take place either before we get out of bed in the morning or a few moments later, might begin with a conscious remembrance of the invisible Presence and Power operating in this universe.

How did this day come to be? Surely, there must be a tremendous Force, Power, Being, or Presence, which has brought forth the sunlight, the rain, or the snow of this day. There is a Something operating invisibly in this universe, sending forth all this glory into expression, a glory of which I am a part, for I, too, have been sent into expression by That which sent forth the flowers and the trees, the birds, and all that is.

I am one with all life. And just as this invisible Force is pouring sunshine into the room, so it is pouring life and being into me, and through me: intelligence, wisdom, guidance, direction, love, care, and protection. All of these are flowing in and through me from the infinite invisible Source.

And so we go through this period of contemplative meditation at least three or four times a day, each time taking some other subject. For the moment, however, we

---

* The italicized portions of this book are spontaneous meditations that have come to the author during periods of uplifted consciousness and are not in any sense intended to be used as affirmations, denials, or formulas. They have been inserted in this book from time to time to serve as examples of the free flowing of the Spirit.

are considering our major theme, which is that we are consciously one with God; we are consciously one with our Creator. We are consciously one with the Source of life, but until we make it a conscious activity, until we consciously realize that we are one with our Source, that we are inseparable and indivisible from infinity and eternality, and that all these qualities and activities are pouring themselves through us—until we *consciously* do this we are not experiencing that which is our birthright. We are children of God, and as children heirs to all the heavenly riches. But let us not think that we are going to come into our heritage without consciously bringing our heritage into expression. It has to be a conscious activity.

Whatever of harmony, joy, or success is to come into our experience must first of all be brought there through some conscious activity of our mind or through a conscious activity of a meditative nature. Some day, the Western world will understand this subject of meditation better than it does today, and even the Eastern countries will have restored to them the knowledge of meditation which has largely been lost in that part of the world. It is not that those of the East have not meditated, but, because they have not known the real secret of meditation, they have not meditated correctly, even though it is in the East that meditation was discovered and has been practiced most widely. With the loss of the art of meditation comes the loss of all that is really worthwhile in life, because this lack of communion with the Father removes us from that conscious oneness with our infinite Source, and when that happens, we are no longer one with our good.

It takes only a very few weeks of devoting a few moments a day to a quiet meditation in which we recognize our oneness with the Source and realize that our oneness with that Source constitutes our oneness with all our good before we begin to perceive in our outer and daily experience the fruitage of that meditation.

Every moment of meditation rewards us richly. Far more will come forth from it than we put into it. On the other hand, nothing will come forth except what we do put into it. For example, the presence of God is closer to us than our own breathing, and this has always been true. If we try to visualize something closer than our own breathing, we shall understand that actually the very presence of God is where we are. When we are in the depths of disease, sin, or lack, at that very second, the presence of God is as available to us as it was to Moses when he was leading the Hebrews out of slavery, or as it was to Elijah when he was finding cakes baked on the stones or a widow supplying him with food. The presence of God is as present with us as it was with Jesus Christ when he healed the sick or when he multiplied the loaves and fishes or forgave sinners, but even so, that presence of God may be doing absolutely nothing for us because the responsibility for bringing it into active expression in our lives rests with us.

The presence of God is on the gallows; the presence of God is on the battlefront where death and destruction are imminent; the presence of God is where every accident occurs anywhere in the world. The presence of God is in all those places and circumstances, but the presence of God is of no avail to anyone except to those who are dwelling in the conscious awareness of this truth. We must abide from morning to night and night to morning in this realization:

Where I am, God is. The presence of God is closer to me than breathing; I and my Father are inseparable and indivisible because we are one. If I mount up to heaven, I will find God, not that I will find God in heaven, but I will take God up to heaven. If I make my bed in hell, I will find God, not because God is in hell, but because I will take God with me; and if I walk through the valley of the shadow of death, I will find God because where I am, God is, and where God is, I am: we are inseparably and indivisibly one.

Those who abide in this realization consciously find that when any form of evil comes into their experience, it dissolves and disappears. This is the secret of the mystical life; this is the secret of the spiritual life. It is all embodied in the one word *consciously*. Those who consciously know the truth are those who experience truth because truth is present, whether or not they know it. Two times two is four, even in the presence of those who do not know it; but to be of any benefit, two times two must be consciously known.

Gratitude and the Contemplative Life

Gratitude is one of the most powerful forces in the life of any individual because it is one of the many facets of love. If we understand the nature of gratitude, we shall find that it will play a far greater part in our experience than we can possibly realize. The mistake of most of the people in the world is that they are grateful for the good that comes to *them*. They are grateful for the bread on *their* table. They say grace, little realizing how much time they are wasting as long as their grace is only a gratitude for the bread on *their* own table.

Gratitude has nothing to do with gratefulness for the good that comes to us. Like everything else in the spiritual life, God is not only universal, but impersonal, in the sense that God is no respecter of persons and never has sent anything to you or to me or given anything to you or to me. All that God has is ours, but if we were to claim that for ourselves alone, we would perhaps lose it. When I say, "All that the Father has is mine," I mean that that same allness is yours and everyone else's. The fact that all the people in the world are not recipients of that good is because of their unawareness—their lack of conscious recognition—of this truth.

In other words, be assured that God has never singled out Joel or anyone else to whom to give anything: not even the message of the Infinite Way. The Infinite Way is an activity of consciousness, and anyone who opens his consciousness to it can experience it, because God is no respecter of persons. God does not set a table for you or for me; God has set a table for this whole universe. God has not put anyone's name tag on the cattle on a thousand hills, the crops in the ground, the pearls in the sea, or the diamonds in the earth. God has not put anyone's name on anything that He has given to this universe: God has expressed Himself universally; God has shown forth His glory universally.

The moment we begin to be grateful just for the fact that God is in His heaven, our lives begin to change. Therefore, let us stop thinking in terms of "me" and "mine" and begin to be grateful for all the good that God has provided in this universe: grateful that crops are in the ground and that the bowels of the earth are filled with His riches, rejoicing in the universality of God's good, rejoicing and being grateful for the riches that are upon the face of this earth, rejoicing that everyone who opens his consciousness to them receives them, not because God sends these things to him but because God sends them out into the world as His presence made manifest.

The presence of God appears as food, clothing, housing, and raiment. All that is, is the presence of God made manifest, and when we begin to express gratitude for the presence of God appearing as the good in this world, our souls, our minds, and our hearts are filled with love. When we personalize and believe that for some reason God has given to one person and is with-holding from another, we dishonor God.

Let it be clear, then, that to our meditation and our practicing of the Presence, we must add the all-important ingredient of gratitude. As we walk in the park, let us be grateful for all the beauty that is on every hand to gladden the heart. If we look up into the sky when the stars are shining, let us be grateful that they are there—but let us be equally careful not to claim the stars for our own!

What concerned me in my earlier years was that so much of God's abundance and love were in evidence and yet that there was so much of poverty, sin, and disease among men. And for me, the burning question was why this was true, and how it could be eliminated. The answer that came was that only through our con-scious awareness and acceptance of God's grace, through consciously living in the realization of God's presence could those things that do not belong in our experience be eliminated and be replaced by those things that are ours by divine right.

For this reason, the two books *Practicing the Presence*[4] and *The Art of Meditation*[5] have been provided as the foundational studies in our work because all our work must necessarily be founded on the ability to meditate consciously and to practice consciously the presence of God until we reach the point where we never go to sleep at night without God in our thought, nor awaken in the morning without God as our first thought. We go forth from our home with God in our thought. We live constantly with God in our thought.

This is the way, then, that the blessings of God reach man: through an activity of our own consciousness, through our consciously knowing the truth and praying without ceasing. And these blessings are all by-products of the one great goal of conscious awareness of the presence of God.

Across the Desk

Everything visible, audible, touchable, smellable, and thinkable is the external expression of something in the realm of the real—even the superstitions, myths, and so-called pagan practices.

As visitors from the Occident go to the Orient and observe the unusually large number of temples, shrines, religious statues, and prayer groups, they often speak of these as the paganism of the Orient. When they return home and in the churches on nearly every corner of every town find even a greater number of prayer groups, many stained glass windows, religious figures, and statues of Jesus in different forms and positions from that of prayer to crucifixion, statues and paintings of saints and sages, I wonder how many of them perceive that all these outward symbols stem from the same source.

Let us be very clear on this point: Behind all the seemingly paganistic practices of the East and the West, there is spiritual truth. First of all, the very existence of a prayer group in a church, temple, or garden is an acknowledgment of a supreme Being or Deity. Whether sitting, standing, or on the knees, through prayer one acknowledges a divine Presence. On this point both East and West are in agreement.

The statues and carvings of religious leaders in the East are a recognition of those whose lives have revealed their attainment of some measure of divine consciousness. The paintings, the stained glass, and the figures in Western churches are but the recognition of the attained measure of spiritual light of the Western Savior, his disciples and apostles, and of other religious lights. Here, too, the East and the West are in agreement, and rightly so, because all religious symbolism in ritual, rite, or ceremony is the attempt to use such means to attain an elevated state of consciousness.

Behind all *forms* of worship, it must be recognized that there is a divine, infinite, universal principle of law, life, or being, and in such recognition it becomes clear that *the Lord He is One*. To the discerning person there is, therefore, no paganism in any religion, and no one can correctly claim that there is a right or a wrong religion. The paganism exists in the form of men's worship and in their differing beliefs about religion. For example, to believe that man can influence God by words, thoughts, or deeds is a form of paganism; whereas to realize God as Omniscience, Omnipotence, and Omnipresence is true religious worship.

To believe that God has finite form, emotions, or responses is a form of paganism; whereas to understand God as the Life, Law, Being, Substance, and Activity of all spiritual form is true worship. To tell God, to advise, inform, or beseech God is a form of paganism; whereas to love and trust God and to listen for His voice is the higher worship.

To have an inner experience of the outer forms of worship such as is carried on in church services or in celebrating religious holidays, feast or fast days, is true worship, and the true worshiper can participate in the services of the Hebrew synagogue, the Protestant or Catholic church, or the Moslem or Buddhist temple with equal devotion, because behind this worship, whatever its form, he recognizes and acknowledges the One "appearing as many."

With equal dedication, I have spoken to Christian groups and non-Christian groups in the Orient, and all of them have listened to me with equal interest and attention. Thus, the Infinite Way bears witness to the divine Spirit in man, the divine Spark which is without race, religion, nationality, creed, or political affiliation, yet is the one animating Principle, Life, Soul, and Spirit of all. In this oneness, there is a spiritual bond uniting us in His grace.

~ 2 ~

ERASING OUR CONCEPTS OF GOD, PRAYER, AND GRACE

Religion is an individual experience, and not only is it impossible to go into heaven two by two or four by four, but even any attempt to do so must result in failure.

If a person is interested in a spiritual way of life, in seeking the realm of God or finding a solution to human problems, it is necessary that that person embark on his mission alone. This does not mean that if one's husband or wife also wishes to set forth on such a mission he or she should not do so, but because of the very nature of this search, each one must find his way within himself, alone. No two people can progress at the same rate because no two people are at the same level of consciousness; and therefore, the religious life is one which must be lived within the individual, regardless of how much is shared outwardly. No one can achieve this life for another: each must achieve it for himself.

In the writings and recordings of the Infinite Way is found the account of my own search for God: the mode, the means, and the achievement. This has been set forth merely to show what one individual has achieved, and these books and recordings are offered to you in the hope that you will read, study, or hear them, and put them into practice; and, insofar as they prove successful, live with them and through them.

In a few brief years, many thousands who have followed the particular way known as the Infinite Way have, in a measure, found their peace, their harmony, safety, security, and their supply. In reading and studying the Infinite Way, however, you are in no sense bound to it. You are, at all times, a free spiritual agent, free to come to us or to any of our students who are active in the work, but just as free at any time not to come—always free to find your own way. You have no obligations; you have no embarrassments; and if the Infinite Way does not prove effective in your individual case, you are at liberty always to seek further until you do find the particular teaching which is yours.

You are under no obligation to me or to the message of the Infinite Way. There is nothing you can join, so there are no memberships or ties to dissolve. Come, enjoy, eat, drink, be satisfied, but let each one of us maintain his oneness with God. In such a way lies true freedom, true liberty, and the obligation each one has is to his Maker and not to any man. What a satisfying thing that is to remember!

Day and night and night and day, I owe no man anything but to love him. My sole obligation is to love my God and my fellow man. There is no way of expressing the joy and the freedom this gives all of us; there is no way of explaining what takes place in the consciousness of an individual who knows that he is free in God.

When people come together in large groups, there is a tendency to rely on that togetherness, or that union, for their demonstration of peace, harmony, and security, and they thereby lose. The idea that in union there is strength has been drilled into people from infancy, but this is not true, except in the spiritual sense of union with God, not union with one another.

Couples have married, believing that in such union would be their strength and later have found that each had to find his or her strength individually—that strength could not be found collectively. Nations have united, but these unions have usually lasted only as long as they have not interfered with or jeopardized the selfish aims and ambitions of the parties involved.

When people unite humanly for the purpose of finding safety, security, peace, harmony, or health, they must fail because the only way to achieve these is in the degree of their oneness with God, consciously realized—their oneness with their Source. That is something that no one can do for another. Each must achieve this for himself.

No Theory or Concept of God Is God

There is a difficulty in embarking on a spiritual way of life, and one which everyone has to surmount if he is to remain on the spiritual path. That difficulty concerns itself with three words, but once you are able to rise above the limitations of those three words, you will find that the spiritual path is much easier than you had ever believed it could be, and much more joyous and fruitful. For a time, however, the struggle lies in these three words, the first of which is God—G-o-d.

The hardest part of your spiritual journey is to rise above the concepts of God that you have always accepted. Whether your concept of God has come from a church, from your parents, or from your own experiences in life—regardless of where or how you acquired your particular concept of God and regardless of what that concept may be—it is not God.

There is nothing that you know about God that is God. There is no idea of God that you can entertain that is God. There is no possible thought that you can have about God that is God. It makes no difference what your idea may be or what your concept may be, it remains an idea or a concept, and an idea or a concept is not God. And so every student must eventually realize that he has to rise above all his concepts of God before he can have an experience of God.

Regardless of the concept of God entertained, whether Hebrew, Protestant, Catholic, or Oriental, it has done very little for the world. This world is in a sad plight, and every known concept of God has failed to bring peace on earth—not only collectively, but individually.

The world is in a state of unrest because of fear of aggression on the part of Russia and China or because of the upheaval in Africa. The threat to world peace arising out of the situation in these areas would not of itself be too upsetting to anyone, except for the fact that very few persons have within themselves that which makes them independent of world conditions. In other words, they have no assurance within themselves that there is a God who can and will lift them out of these world problems and show them how to surmount them.

Just in one generation, there have been three major wars, and neither the Hebrew, the Protestant, the Catholic, nor the Oriental God has stopped these wars or their horrors. They never ended until one or the other of the combatants had nothing left with which to fight.

For the most part, men feel that they have nothing within themselves that can give them any assurance that, regardless of human conditions, the evils of war, poverty, or disease will not come nigh their dwelling place.

The answer to all this is that whatever concept of God a person may entertain or however correct that concept may be, it still will not give him freedom, peace, safety, or security. Only one thing will bring these things to an individual, and ultimately to the world, and that one thing is the God-experience: not a theory about God, not a concept of God, not an idea of God, but a God-experience!

For nearly two thousand years, religion has eliminated that factor from its teaching. It has given the world everything *but* the God-experience: it has given it noble ideas; it has given it great ideas of philanthropy and charity; it has given it great beauty in music, art, and literature—everything, in fact, except God. But we could well dispense with all that religion has given us, if only it would give us God. We can live without all these other things, if only we can have God.

The attainment of God is an individual experience and cannot be given to a group of individuals, although it may be given to many individuals in a group. It is possible at a given time for a dozen persons in a group to realize God, but they will not receive that realization as a group. Each one receives it individually by his own preparedness for it, by his own devotion to the attainment of God-realization.

Healing Comes Through in a Moment
of God-Realization

Those of you who, in the capacity of practitioner or teacher, have been the means of spiritual healing for others are well aware of the fact that you do not know how to heal and that you have no healing powers or capacities. You know, better than anyone else, that the Master was right when he said, "I can of mine own self do nothing,"[1] that he spoke truly when he said, "If I bear witness of myself, my witness is not true,"[2] because you have found that the only time you have been responsible for healings has been when, in some measure, in your meditation or treatment, you have actually felt a Presence or a release from fear, which could not have come except by the grace of God. Only when you attained a certain level of consciousness, a very specific level of consciousness, in which you either realized God's presence or realized the absolute nothingness of anything that was not ordained of God, have you ever been able to bring forth healing.

To those of you who have experienced healings through a practitioner or teacher of the metaphysical or spiritual world, let me say that the healing did not take place because God was favoring that practitioner or teacher and conferring upon him special healing powers. The healing had nothing to do with anything of this sort. It had to do with the fact that the one to whom you turned was able to catch a glimpse of the God-presence or power, of the spiritual nature of creation, or a realization of the nonpower of anything and everything that does not emanate from God. It is in such moments of realization that healing comes through.

So it is that those who expect only to be healed should, of course, in some degree try to realize the nature of God, but those of you who engage in an active healing ministry must understand that all your knowledge of truth is of no value when the chips are down. In other words, when you are faced with a person threatened with death or with an incurable disease, do not rely on the wisdom or on the statements of truth you have read or learned in books or lessons. Rather understand that unless you realize and feel God's presence, or unless you actually feel the nothingness of that which is presenting itself as the appearance, the healing will not take place.

Statements of truth and learning the correct letter of truth are necessary steps in our progress, of course, because it is in this way that the healing consciousness is attained, but too much attention is usually given to statements of truth and not enough to the actual experience of truth.

Prayers That Seek Favors of God Are Futile

The concept of God that most persons entertain is that God is a great power and that God can overcome all negative and erroneous powers, that God can heal disease, that God could, if He would, stop a war or prevent accidents. None of this is true; none of this is true!

And that brings us to the second word, the second stumbling block in our progress, the word *prayer*. As long as men and women pray to God to heal the sick, to give them supply, or to bring peace on earth, they are just playing around with marbles. They are not even seriously approaching the subject of spiritual living. Rather are they back in paganistic days, praying those ancient prayers of "O God! Destroy my enemy"; "O God! Give me success in battle"; "O God! Save our side—be with us." All of this dates back two, three, four, or five thousand years to those days when people thought of God as some kind of superman who sat high up on a throne and could be prevailed upon to destroy their enemies and, at the same time, give them success. Why success to them and not to their enemies?

Similarly, prayers were uttered: "Give us rain"; or, "Stop this too much rain"; "Give us crops"; "Let us have more abundant fish in our nets"; "Make the game more plentiful." Prayer of this sort belongs to those pagan days in which the concept of God was that of some kind of super-being who was sitting around waiting to be persuaded to grant favors.

Such prayers were not effective then, and they have not been effective during the past two thousand years in which they have been perpetuated by the churches. But the world continues to use these outmoded forms of prayer and to live with outmoded concepts of God for much the same reason that contemporaries of Christopher Columbus, once they had gone on record publicly as having accepted a square world, found it difficult to acknowledge that after all perhaps Columbus was right, and the world was round. In spite of knowledge to the contrary, they insisted on clinging to their square world. And so it is that once people have come out publicly and declared that it is right and proper to pray to God to destroy their enemies or to pray to God for bread, meat, wine, and water, it is a very difficult thing for them to admit that they were wrong.

One day it will be recognized that in this twentieth century an era has begun in which concepts of God and prayer will have to be re-examined universally as well as individually. There are many places around the globe in which it is evident that a beginning in this direction has been made.

But we are dealing now only with you and with me as individuals, and if we expect to enter this spiritual path,

it must be done by recognizing that God is
Claus, and Santa Claus is not God. God is not \
ing anything that you could pray for. God has no\
give you that God is not, at this moment, giving.
God whose kingdom is within you already knows y
need, and it is His good pleasure to give you that
Kingdom.

Therefore, the first step on the spiritual path is to
acknowledge that you need not pray to God in the sense
of telling or asking God for what you need because God
is an all-knowing God, an infinite Wisdom that already
knows all that is to be known, and that God is divine
love, whose nature it is to give you the Kingdom.

The Is-ness of God

You cannot know what God is because no one in the
history of the world has ever been able to embrace God
by means of his human mentality. King Solomon said
that his entire Temple was not big enough to hold God,
and you may be assured that the mind of man is not
capable of embracing God. So, it is useless to try to ask
what God is. Rather acknowledge that God *is*.

Acknowledge that as you have looked out upon this
universe and witnessed the orderly movement of the
sun, the moon, the stars, and the tides, and the unfailing
rotation of the seasons, as you have witnessed the divine
order in apple trees producing apples and rosebushes
producing roses, you must admit that there is a Cause
that operates through law and through love.

When you have acknowledged that this universe has
a creative Principle, a Cause, a Something that sent it into
expression and form and that maintains that expression,

this relieves you, individually, of all responsibility. It enables you to relax and realize that that which sent you into expression must likewise be that which maintains and sustains you and all mankind.

Once you have acknowledged that God is, and that God is that which functions as Law, as Love, and as the creative, maintaining, and sustaining Principle, you have set yourself free of all concepts of God and you can rest in that acknowledgment. You can rest assured that that which is maintaining the integrity of all nature can maintain the integrity of your and my individual life.

The Prayer of Acknowledgment

By this time, you will have begun to wonder, "What has happened to the kind of prayers I used to pray?" and you will realize that they have dropped away from you. Now you will know that your acknowledgment of God as the creative and maintaining Principle is about as high a form of prayer as man can conceive of in the realm of words or thoughts. In other words, to acknowledge that there is an infinite Something, even though invisible, to acknowledge Its qualities of intelligence, law, and love, and to acknowledge Its power as the sustaining influence, this is prayer: this is the prayer of acknowledgment.

"In all thy ways acknowledge him, and he shall direct thy paths."[3] Acknowledge this, and eventually you will be elevated to a state of consciousness in which you will pray without words and without thoughts, because after you have received this conviction of a Divinity, of a divine Presence, Power, Law, and Love, there are no more words. You have no words to address to It, but rather you have come to realize that God, whatever Its nature or being, can speak to you, reveal Itself to you, and bring you an assurance of Its presence, Its power, Its jurisdiction and government in all things.

When you become receptive to that God whose Kingdom is within, you will arrive at a point of recognition:

The kingdom of God is within me. I do not have to go to holy mountains; I do not have to go to holy temples or holy cities because the place whereon I stand is holy ground.

With that assurance, you can then turn quietly within and realize:

"Speak, Lord; for thy servant heareth."[4] I know now that it would be folly for human wisdom to try to instruct the Divine. I know now that it would be folly to ask God for anything, as if God were withholding from me.

I know now that I need only be receptive and responsive to God's grace, that I need only turn within and wait and be patient, and the presence of God will announce Itself, and when He utters His voice, the earth melts. When I hear the still small voice, the discords of human sense dissolve.

I know now that "I can of mine own self do nothing."[5] It is only as I can bring forth the presence and the power of God through my consciousness and release it into this world that it is possible to say to the storm, as did the Master, "Peace, be still.[6] . . . It is I; be not afraid."[7]

Regardless of the pictures that present themselves to you—the sins, the lack, limitations, injustices, and inequalities—you do not fight them. You do not pray to a god to do something about them, but you turn within in the realization that the presence of God is within you, and in that quietness and stillness, you hear: "*I* will never leave thee, nor forsake thee.'[8] As *I* * was with Moses, with Abraham, Isaac, Jacob, and Jesus, so *I* am with you. *I* will be with you unto the end of the world."

In one way or another, you will reach an inner confidence that you are not alone in this world, that you are not battling your problems alone, but that it is literally true that He that is within you is greater than he that is in the world and that He performs whatever is given you to do.

These statements as mere statements will do nothing for you except to serve as reminders of the truth that really is. There is a *He* within you that is greater than all the problems that are in the world. There is a *He* that actually performs all that is given you to do. Scriptural or inspirational passages merely give you the confidence to become still and let that *He* come into expression, let that *He* bring you the assurance:

"It is I; be not afraid.[9] *. . . I will never leave thee. "*[10] I *will be with thee.* I *will go before thee to make the crooked places straight.* I *go before thee to reveal mansions—mansions, mansions.* I *am the way—rest.* I *am the truth—rest.*

Do not struggle for what you shall eat, or what you shall drink, or wherewithal you shall be clothed, for I *am your meat, your wine, and your water.*

Eventually, you will understand that your prayers have not been answered because you have been expecting

---

*The word "I," italicized, refers to God.

God to send you health, and this cannot be. God is the only health there is, and the only way to have health is to have God. God is the health of your countenance; therefore, have God, and you will have health. God is your meat, your bread, your wine, your water; therefore, God cannot give you these and God cannot send you these. *God is these,* and the only way that you can permanently and abundantly have bread, meat, wine, and water is to have God.

It is useless to pray to God for longer life, for God cannot give it to you. God is life, and only in having God do you have life. Without God, there is no life, for God is life. And to know this truth is life eternal.

Do not even pray to God for safety or for security, for God has none to give you: God is the fortress, and God is the high tower, and if you want safety and security, have God. When you are in God, and God is in you, you will have no need of concrete shelters; you will have no need of swords, nor will you have fear of anyone else's swords. No individual who has ever had the assurance of God's presence ever fears death, ever fears bombs or bullets because with the realization of God's presence comes the conviction:

Neither life nor death can separate me from God. Neither life nor death can separate me from the love and the care of God. Neither life nor death can separate me from God's life, God's supply, God's Soul, God's law, God's love; and therefore, I need not concern myself with whether my status is life or death, because either way I am in God. God can never leave me, nor forsake me; God is with me to the end of the world because God and I are one, inseparable and indivisible.

Preparing the Soil for Spiritual Fruitage

This assurance cannot be given to us from a book, even though we may read comforting passages there; and this assurance cannot even be given to us by a man, even though we may hear him speak words of faith and trust. This assurance must come welling up in us from within ourselves. That is what I mean by preparation. Those of us who are devoting some part of our day and night to God-realization are preparing ourselves for this very revelation or assurance that inevitably comes from within. Paul told us that as creatures, that is, as human beings, we are not under the law of God, neither indeed can be. It is only as we prepare ourselves that this inner confidence and conviction eventually dawn.

The Master gave it to us this way: there are three types of soil: the barren soil, the rocky, and the fertile. As human beings, we are the barren soil, entirely separate and apart from God, and God has no way at all of announcing Himself within us; there is no way for the revelation of God to come to us.

After we have started out on our spiritual path, it is not long before we find that we have become stony soil. In other words, we do have realizations of truth occasionally; we have revelations and demonstrations; we have a glimpse of something, and then it is gone from us. It does not remain with us too long. We have a demonstration of harmony, and then all of a sudden that seems to be far in the past. But as we continue to abide in the Word and let the Word abide in us, as we continue to seek for deeper and deeper revelations and realizations of God and prayer, eventually we find that we are becoming more fertile soil, and the seed of truth can now take root in us.

Every word of truth that we read, every word of truth that we hear, every word of truth that we declare is a seed of truth, and the further we go in our study and meditations, the more fertile our consciousness becomes and the more of these seeds will take root and bear fruit.

We all go through much the same experience—everyone in the past has gone through these same experiences—but eventually we all come to the realization that to know Him aright is life eternal. This, I would call the greatest revelation ever given to man: *To know Him aright is life eternal:* life harmonious, life perfect.

But let us understand what it means to know Him aright. To know Him aright means to drop every concept we have ever had. The Master said that we cannot fill vessels already full; we have to empty out the vessel, come with a perfectly clear and clean consciousness, and begin all over again.

When our prayer is, "Father, reveal Thyself," we should remember that we are speaking to a Father that is already within us, not a Father that we have to go out and seek, not a God that is afar off. We are beginning with the realization that what we are seeking is already within us. Therefore, we can do our praying, whether we are at business, or doing housework; we can do our praying or our knowing of the truth, whether we are walking, driving a car, or riding in a bus. We can literally pray without ceasing, because regardless of the activity in which we may be engaged, there is always room in our consciousness for a remembrance, for a realization, of God within us.

The Universality of God's Grace

There is a third word about which there are many misconceptions, and that is the word *grace*. God's grace is not given to some and withheld from others. God's grace is free to everyone. God's grace is within us, and it is operating within us, needing only to be recognized.

What stops us from receiving God's grace is that while once a week we may say with our lips, "Thy grace is my sufficiency in all things," ninety-nine other times during the week we plead, "Give me food; give me clothing; give me housing; give me employment; give me companionship." Ninety-nine times out of a hundred, we deny the truth that we utter the one time; whereas the whole one hundred times we should refrain from desiring anything from God, putting our entire hope in this truth:

Thy grace is my sufficiency in all things, and Thy grace is operative and operating now.

It will help to remember that when it rains it does not rain exclusively for the Jones family, the Browns, or the Smiths. When it rains, it just rains. When it snows, it snows; when it is warm, it is warm; and when God is passing out food, clothing, housing, raiment, companionship, and money, it is not for Jones, Brown, or Smith: it is universal. God's grace is universally available. As long as we do not personalize it and expect God to give or send it to us, we will have His grace infinitely and eternally. It is only when we begin to localize it and ask God to let it rain in our garden that we are likely to find that it misses our garden.

God's grace is universal, and God's grace is our sufficiency. God's grace governs the universe, but God's grace is not addressed to anyone except to the Son of God, which you are and which I am. Let us have no addresses to which God's grace is to be sent because God is not interested in one person more than in another.

Let us revise our concepts of prayer and, above all things, let us realize that we cannot pray for something for ourselves, for our child, or for our parents. Our prayer has to be a realization of the omnipresence of God, omnipresent in Russia and Africa and the United States. The omnipresence of God—the omnipotence of God—the omniscience of God—universal, impersonal, impartial! Once we begin to pray this kind of prayer, we shall begin to experience answered prayer.

God's grace cannot be directed into specific channels; God's grace cannot be directed to certain persons: God's grace already is operating universally, and what brings it into our experience is our acknowledgment and realization of its universality. As we begin to understand the universal nature of God's grace, God's love, and God's wisdom, and stop attempting to channel it, we shall begin to perceive that we, ourselves, are inside God's grace, and the beneficiary of it.

Across the Desk

Grace is God's gift of Himself; Grace is omnipresence: it is the impartation of God to an individual in realization, but the realization of God constitutes the receptivity to Grace. God's gift of grace is never a thing or a condition, but always the fullness of God, although our limited state of receptivity may make it appear as a specific healing—as supply or release from some form of bondage. If God's grace appears in limited form, it is usually because we are seeking some specific good.

When we rightly understand the Infinite Way, we seek the realization of the fullness of God—the fulfillment of God.

In turning within daily for the acknowledgment and awareness of God's presence, the effect of God's grace soon becomes apparent as the appearing of the activity and forms of good in our experience. The desire for specific gifts of God must be surrendered in the greater love for God, which is satisfied with nothing less than Himself. Our lives cannot be complete until we have received the Grace of His presence. Then we live constantly tabernacled with Him, in continuous communion with His life and His love.

Men seek many freedoms: freedom from false appetites, from disease, from lack, and from unhappy human relationships, but instead of seeking freedom from these limiting conditions, they should rather seek freedom in His Spirit because freedom is attained by His grace—by the attainment of His presence. If the desire for His grace is strong enough, the struggle for these freedoms can be given up and thereby real freedom attained.

In our morning meditation, we can consciously remember: "I will never leave thee, nor forsake thee"[11]; and in our evening meditation, "Lo, I am with you alway, even unto the end of the world."[12] And throughout the day, as the pressure of living pushes down upon us, we can inwardly sing: "I am come that they might have life, and that they might have it more abundantly."[13] We can pause at each meal to remember inwardly: Thy grace is my sufficiency in all things. Whenever any sense of bondage tries to tempt us, we can rejoice that "Where the Spirit of the Lord is, there is liberty."[14]

The main concern of the world today is with reports of repeated threats to every kind of freedom—political, religious, and economic—yet none of these evils shall "come nigh [our] dwelling,"[15] if we dwell consciously in the realization of His presence.

To bring to fruition the dawning in consciousness of His grace, we must remember the major principle of life: There is but one Power, and this Power is within us. There is no external power to act upon us or our affairs for *all* power is spiritual, and its kingdom, its realm, is within us. Thou, Pilate—of any name or nature—can have no power except that which is of God.

Fear not—*I* am with you.

~ 3 ~

BEGINNING THE CONTEMPLATIVE LIFE

In the Orient, as many of you know, those who are interested in attaining spiritual illumination go to a teacher and, as a rule, live with or near the teacher for a period of six, seven, or eight years, and by means of meditation with as well as without the teacher, meditation with other students, and spiritual instruction, eventually attain their illumination: *satori,* enlightenment, or the fourth dimensional consciousness.

Mankind as a whole, however, is not geared for this kind of teaching, nor do many desire, need, or even have the capacity for full enlightenment. This is attested by the fact that some students and disciples who have lived in close association with their teachers even for many years could not or did not reach the heights, whereas others may have received it in two or three years.

The question, then, for the young student at first is not one of attaining that degree of illumination which would set him up as a spiritual teacher or healer, but primarily how to attain sufficient illumination or enlightenment to be able to free himself from the discords and inharmonies of daily living and build up within himself a spiritual sense that would not only lift him above the world's troubles–his family or community troubles–but would enable him to live a normal family, business, or

nal life, and yet be inspired, fed, and supported
er experience and contact.

Recognize the Universality of God

It is well known that all people of a religious turn of
mind—whatever their religion may be—can attain some
measure of inner harmony and peace and find themselves in possession of an inner grace that eventually
lives their lives for them. It makes no difference what a
person's religion is because there is only one God, only
one Spirit; and that Spirit knows no difference between
a Jew and a Gentile, a Protestant and a Catholic, an
Oriental and an Occidental. The Spirit is beyond and
above any denominational beliefs or convictions, free to
all and independent of ceremonies, rites, creeds, or
forms for Its worship, just as the life that permeates a
blade of grass is the same life that permeates an orchid,
a daisy, or a violet. The Spirit recognizes no difference.
The same Life animates all life, whether that of a mon-
grel dog or a pedigreed one.

In Scripture, we are told that His rain falls on the just
and the unjust. As far as God is concerned, there is
neither Greek nor Jew, neither bond nor free. The
Master made that very clear when he said, "Call no man
your father upon the earth: for one is your Father, which
is in heaven."[1] If Jesus had meant that this applied only
to the people who were listening to him, then, of course,
according to that, God is the Father only of the Hebrews
because Jesus was talking to his fellow Hebrews. In his
day there was no Christian church, nor were there any
Christians: there were only Jews, and Jesus was one of
them, a rabbi in their midst; and if he had intended

these words only for those to whom he was speaking, we would have to admit, then, that the Jews are the only ones who can claim God as their Father.

As a matter of fact, however, anyone with even a smattering of spiritual insight knows from the import of Jesus' teaching that he was not speaking to any one group. What he was doing was voicing truth, just as if he had said two times two is four while speaking of cabbages, but not meaning that only two times two cabbages is four, but meaning two times two is four, whether applied to cabbages or kings. And so, when he tells us to "call no man your father upon the earth," he is not addressing you who are reading this, nor was he addressing those who were sitting before him listening to him: he was speaking to the world, proclaiming a message that had been given to him of God.

Years later, Paul carried that same message to the pagans, the Europeans—even to the atheists—and always he was voicing a spiritual truth which was not meant to apply to any specific group of people, but was a spiritual truth which has always been, is, and always will be—a universal truth. Therefore, it must be the truth about Greek and Jew; it must be the truth about you and me; it must be the truth about white and black: there is but one Father, but one God.

No person can ever hope for spiritual enlightenment unless he can first of all recognize that there is only one creative Principle in this world, whether It creates cabbages or kings, whether It creates the Greek or the Jew. There is only one creative Principle, and It is located, not in holy mountains, nor yet in the temple in Jerusalem. Its location is neither "Lo here! or, Lo there!"[2] but within you, and it makes no difference who the *you* may be. It makes no difference if it is the you in a hospital, the you in a prison, the you in business, or the you in some art or profession: the kingdom of God is within *you*, and the kingdom of God is a Spirit—not a superhuman being, but a Spirit.

To recognize this truth constitutes the very first step in attaining spiritual light, the first step in attaining an awareness of the presence of God. If you cannot accept this, then you will have to believe that God is a respecter of persons and that only Jews have the presence of God, or only Baptists, or Buddhists. This is the rankest kind of nonsense.

The presence of God is within *you*, whoever the you may be.

Your Givingness of Yourself Brings the Givingness of the Universe to You

When you have come to the place where you actually feel the truth of this, where you feel the presence of God in the air, in your body, in your business, in your home, in your competitor, or in the enemy across the sea or across the street—when you begin to perceive that, you are ready for the next step which everyone must take before enlightenment can come, and that is the realization that inasmuch as the kingdom of God is within you, it must be permitted to flow out from you. It cannot come to you, and you must, at some stage in your unfoldment, stop looking for it to come to you.

An illustration of this can be found in the area of companionship. Many, many persons are seeking companionship, but when they come to me with that problem, asking for a demonstration of companionship, my reply always is: "It's no use, because I know you don't want companionship. If I could show you how to attain it, you would refuse it. What you want is a companion, and probably he has to be five foot eleven to six feet, and weigh one hundred eighty pounds, and have nice blue eyes. You have it all decided in advance. But companionship, you don't want." No one who ever asks for a demonstration of companionship—not anyone I have ever known—has really wanted it. They have merely wanted a companion, and that I cannot get for anybody.

It is so simple to have companionship. All it requires is that you be a companion. That's all! Once you become a companion, once you find something or somebody to companion with—it does not have to be a human being at first, or a member of the opposite sex, or a stranger—you have companionship. You can begin to find companionship with some members of your own family, or with the birds that come to your lawn, or with the stars. The point is that companionship is a sharing of one's self. That is what constitutes companionship—the sharing of one's self. It could be at the level of neighborliness; it could be at the level of friendliness; it could be at the level of husband, wife, brother, or sister; but companionship means a sharing of one's self with someone else.

Companionship is always available to you, because it is within you: it is the gift of God, and you are the one who determines whether you will keep it locked up within you, or whether you will let it loose and be a companion. And the moment you decide to be a companion, you have companionship.

Of course, the wonderful part of it is that when you begin to be a companion, you find those who are also desirous of being companions, of sharing, and then it is not a question of give and take, it is a question of both giving. There is no taking: there is just giving.

The kingdom of God is locked up within you. There is no way for one person to demonstrate supply for another because everyone, everywhere, has all that the Father has—infinity—and to try to get something out here, when there is nothing out here but space, is folly. Supply is demonstrated, not in the getting, but in opening out a way for the supply already within you to flow out from its Source, which is the kingdom of God within you.

Illumination can come only to those who realize that the kingdom of God—Light, Truth, Wisdom, Love—is within. All that the Father has is yours, and then just as you have to find a way to express companionship, so do you have to find a way to express supply.

This we can do in many ways. The Master has indicated in the Sermon on the Mount that we should give, but be sure that no one but God knows about our giving; pray, but be sure that no one but God knows about our praying; forgive; pray for our enemies. All this he gives as an activity that takes place within ourselves and knows from within us to the without.

The entire secret of spiritual illumination is bound up in the realization that the kingdom of God is within and that we must find a way to let this "imprisoned splendor" escape. Therefore, whatever it is we are seeking, we must find a way to give it out, so that even if we are seeking spiritual light, the way to gain it is to give it.

Many teachers have discovered that by the end of the school term, they have learned more about the subjects they have taught through the teaching of them than have the pupils in the classroom. Always a person learns more by teaching than anyone ever learns by being taught.

So it is in a spiritual teaching. Those who teach learn far more than any student or group of students, because in the very act of giving out, there is a constant inflow—and really not in! it is only that the infinite Source is within, but It cannot flow out if we do not let It out. The moment we begin letting out a little of what we know, all the rest begins to flow, more than we ever were aware that we knew.

There is no way to gain love from the world or from the people of the world. Many have tried it, but everyone fails. It cannot be accomplished. The only way is the way of spiritual light. By loving, we become loved. There is no other way. Waiting to be loved is like waiting for something to come from the blankness of space. Before love can flow to us, we first must put it out here. We must first put the bread on the water, before the bread can return to us. Only that which we put forth finds its way back to us, because, in and of itself, a blank space has nothing to give—nothing! But in proportion as we put something out into space, in that proportion is a way made for it to find its way back to us, pressed down and running over.

So is the whole goodness and infinity of this universe flowing back to us as we let it flow out from us. It is the givingness of ourselves that brings the givingness of the universe to us.

Man Cannot Influence God

Spiritual illumination begins with the realization of as simple a thing as that the whole kingdom of God is already established within you, and for you to enjoy its blessings you have to find a way to bring it forth into expression.

As you meditate and ponder on these things, you come to a place where there is nothing more to think about. You have thought it all; you have said it all; you have declared or affirmed it, and you have come to the end of all that. Now, since there is not anything more to say, you come to a place where you are still, and you find that in the very moment that you achieve stillness, something jumps up here from within you—something of a transcendental nature, something of a not human nature. Something jumps up into your awareness that you yourself have not been declaring, affirming, or stating, but which you are now hearing and receiving from the depths of your withinness. You yourself have created the circumstance by means of which this transcendental hearing can take place: you have known the truth, declared it, felt it, stated it, and then been still, thereby creating a vacuum, and now up into that, the Voice announces Itself, bringing with It illumination.

The first step is always consciously knowing the truth, intellectually knowing the truth, and then, through this constant pondering, meditating, and cogitating, you bring yourself to the place where you are completely still, and into that stillness and up from that stillness comes the very light that you have been seeking.

But do you think that that light is given only to one person or one group of persons? Do you not see how important it is, first, to divest yourself of every bit of belief that God is a respecter of persons, of religions, or of churches, or a respecter of races, and come to see clearly that God is a Spirit, that God is life, that God is love, that actually the presence of God is within you?

The very place whereon you stand is holy ground because the presence of God is there. But when you are declaring that about yourself, look up, look around you, and see all the hundreds of people in your neighborhood, and then remember that whether or not they know this truth, you must know that it is the truth about them, because if you are not knowing this truth as a universal truth, you are again trying to pinch a little of it off for yourself, to make it finite or limit it, and God cannot be limited.

The next step is easier now than it would have been but for the two previous steps, namely, (1) knowing the truth, and (2) realizing that God is no respecter of persons. Now you are better able to recognize that man cannot influence God, that man has no power over God's creation, man has no jurisdiction over God's world, man has no jurisdiction over God, period. Man cannot have his way with God; man cannot get God to do his will or his way; and therefore, the next need is to become a beholder because, since you cannot influence God, you can at least watch what God is doing. You can become a witness to the activity of God in your life and everybody else's life because, remember, when the sun comes up in the morning, it comes up for Jew and Gentile, white and black, Oriental and Occidental: it has no favorites; and you have to be willing to recognize that just as the sun rises for everybody in the whole world, so is God's grace available to everybody in the world.

When you watch sugar cane or pineapples growing, it is foolish to think that God is growing them for you or for me. God is just growing them. God's grace falls on the just and the unjust.

Always there must be the remembrance, then, that what God is doing, God is doing, and He does not need your help; and furthermore He cannot be controlled by you or me or by anybody else. God's grace cannot be stopped. Even if you think that you are acting in disobedience to His laws, God's grace is still flowing, even though you may not get the benefit of it because you have cut yourself off from it.

"Whatsoever a man soweth, that shall he also reap."[3] God has nothing to do with your sowing or your reaping. It is as *you* sow: "He that soweth to his flesh shall of the flesh reap corruption; but he that soweth to the Spirit shall of the Spirit reap life everlasting."[4] It is always what *you* do. By your thoughts and actions of today, you determine your reaping of tomorrow.

So therefore, even if by some act of your own— whether it is a disobedience to one or more of the Ten Commandments, or whether it is a violation of the second great commandment of the Master to love your neighbor as yourself, or whatever it is—if you have shut off health, safety, security, and inner peace, do not blame God for it, for God neither gives you peace nor takes it from you; God neither gives you health nor takes it from you; God neither gives you supply nor takes it from you. God's grace is as free as sunshine. If you like, you can pull down the shades and never see the sun, and never feel it, but that is because of your action, not God's. As far as God is concerned, the sunshine is always there.

So it is, then, that in the moment when you realize that God's grace is very much like the sun hanging in the sky, it is there; it is available for everyone, even though, temporarily, there may be clouds hiding it, but nevertheless, it is there. Your very recognition of this and your refusal to try to get God to do something, your ability to refrain from entreating or begging God, from attempting to influence or bribe Him, the very act itself of refraining from doing these things brings the activity of God into your experience.

When you can sit back and realize that God is—not because of you, but that actually in spite of you, still God is closer to you than breathing, the place whereon you stand is holy ground, and where the presence of the Lord is, there is freedom and fulfillment—when you learn to refrain from attempting to take heaven by storm, and when you are able to sit back in the realization, "Where I am, God is," and be still, you have opened the way in your own consciousness for the Omnipresence which is already there to make Itself manifest and evident in your experience.

The great error has always been trying to influence God: "God, go out there and destroy my enemies! God, go out there and bring my enemies' possessions to me!" This attempt to personalize God or to get God to do something for some specific person and not for everybody indicates a lack of understanding of God as Spirit.

The very statement that God is Spirit is in itself a freeing and a healing one. No one can do anything about moving or changing Spirit, influencing It or bribing It. There is nothing to do but *let* It envelop you, *let* It pick you up, *let* It dominate *you, let* Its will be done in you, and then you make of yourself a transparency through which the light that is already present within you can shine: not a light that is gained from books or from some form of worship, or from teachers, but a light that books or worship or teachers can reveal to you as already having existence within you.

The teacher's function is to unveil the light that already constitutes your innermost being, self, or identity. The function of the teacher and the teaching is to unveil the presence of the Spirit of God that is within you, so that you can eventually live in this conviction, "Thank You, Father; You and I are one."

What the Master has said is true: "I will never leave thee, nor forsake thee.[5] . . . Lo, I am with you always, even unto the end of the world,"[6] but the teacher unveils and reveals to you the Presence that is saying this to you from within your own being and reminding you that the Father knows your need before you do. It is His good pleasure to give you the Kingdom. Therefore, you can rest in this realization: *The Father is within me. The kingdom of God is within me.*

The Indwelling Presence

There is a divine Presence within you, and it is the function of this Presence to heal the sick, raise the dead, preach the Gospel, feed the hungry, and forgive sinners: this is Its function. It has never left you—It will never leave you! You could change your religion seven times over, but that Presence would still be with you. You could live in a place where no one had ever heard of a church, and the Presence would still be with you. It will *never* leave you, nor forsake you. And remember this: It is not dependent upon anything. It is not even dependent upon your having a right thought. It is always there, but your enjoying the benefits of It is dependent upon your knowing the truth of Its omnipresence.

Gradually, as you receive confirmation from within yourself that it is true that there is a Presence, the Voice speaks to you. Whether It speaks audibly or not is of no importance, as long as in one way or another you feel that you are living by Grace, not by might, not by power, not by force, but by Grace, by a divine Grace that operates just as freely as the incoming and outgoing tides or the rising and the setting of the sun, and just as painlessly. It is not a matter of earning or deserving it.

As human beings, we can never earn or deserve the grace of God, and that is why we are told that we must *die daily* and that we must be reborn of the Spirit. The truth is that as children of God we are heirs to God's grace, and all we have to do is to recognize our sonship.

And so as we ponder these basic truths, as we learn to come into a state of mind, a state of consciousness, that is filled with an assurance that there is an inner Presence, and learn to relax in It, we find that It does our thinking for us; It corrects and enlightens us; It goes before us to make the crooked places straight; It is a healing influence in mind and body; It is a supplying presence. But It does all this without any help from us, except for our ability to relax in It.

"He maketh me to lie down in green pastures: he leadeth me beside the still waters"[7]—it is always *He*. "He performeth the thing that is appointed for me"[8]—not the little "I," but *He*. "The Lord will perfect that which concerneth me."[9] But do you not see that He cannot do it if we take hold of the reins and do all the driving? If we take thought for what we shall eat, or what we shall drink, or wherewithal we shall be clothed, we are leaving no room for any *He:* it is all that little "I," the very "I" that should be *dying daily* in order that that *I* which is our spiritual identity can be reborn.

If you have grasped what I have said up to this point, you should be able to understand the passage, "In quietness and in confidence shall be your strength"[10]—in quietness and in confidence. How can you be quiet, how can you have confidence unless you have this awareness of an inner Grace? And you can only have this awareness of an inner Grace when you begin to recognize Its universal nature, recognize that It belongs to all men.

Those who are not recognizing this inner Grace, we are told, are the thousand that fall at our left and the ten thousand at our right, those, as the Master tells us, who are not abiding in the Word nor letting the Word abide in them and who, therefore, are as a branch of a tree that is cut off and withereth.

So it is that not everybody will benefit by this truth just because it is the truth. No! Only "ye" who know the truth permit the truth to make you free—you who abide in this Word of an indwelling Presence. Those of you who stop—I was going to say stop annoying God, but I am sure that God cannot be annoyed—those of you who stop going through the motions that would annoy God, if God could be annoyed, that is, trying to influence Him, trying to bribe Him, trying to promise Him something in the future, instead of realizing that God is Spirit, God is life, God is love, and that you have to find a way to let all of this flow out from you, will come into an actual awareness of the presence of God.

The Contemplative Life Develops a Sense of Universality

This really constitutes a way of life. True, it is a religious way of life, except that if you use such a term, it would seem to denote some particular religion with special rituals and ceremonies, and it is not that kind of life at all. It is a religious life in the sense that this teaching develops a conscious awareness of God, but to avoid giving the impression that we have found some particular religion through which God is blessing us, we should rightly call this the contemplative way of life because it is a way of life that can be lived by all people regardless of any personal or denominational persuasion.

The contemplative way of life recognizes God as Spirit, and that Spirit as Omnipresence—the Spirit within one's own being. Therefore, it is an absolutely unrestricted way of life, available to anyone of any faith or no faith, as long as he can recognize that God is Spirit, recognize God as its central theme—not your God or my God, just God—and a God that belongs to nobody, a God that just is, and is universal.

That is why the contemplative life can flourish in every country on the globe where there is freedom and where people are not compelled to worship in a specific way. Even where there is no freedom, this way of life can be followed because it does not build a fence around God or lay down specific rules: it just recognizes God as the Principle of life, the Grand Architect of the whole universe.

For this reason, then, the contemplative life is the way for any person who can recognize that wherever or however God is worshiped, it is the same God, that there cannot be more than one God. Whether as Hebrews we go into a temple with hats on, or as Christians with hats off, as Orientals with our shoes off or as Christians with shoes on, it must be understood that these outward forms can make no difference, that all we are doing is worshiping in whatever way means dedication or sacredness to us.

What represents sacredness to an individual determines his worship. If an individual feels that he is honoring God by keeping his hat on, that is merely his idea of worship and sanctity, but the act of wearing or not wearing a head covering does not change God. If another individual feels that he is honoring God with his shoes off, that very act is an evidence of the sincerity of that individual's worship. Therefore, when you live the contemplative life, you will respect the Moslem who takes off his shoes and sits on the ground, and you will respect those who have other ceremonial forms of worship, and you will also respect those who have no form of worship at all, because you will know that each in his own way is dedicating himself to God, and not his God because God is not the possession of any one person: there is only God, and God is Spirit.

The contemplative, then, is actually paving the way for world peace, because he is recognizing that there is only one Father, one God, equally of all, and that all men everywhere are brothers and sisters; and therefore, the only relationship that is essential is that we treat each other as members of one united household.

To do this is to love the one and only God supremely, but it is also to love your neighbor as yourself. When you acknowledge one God as Father and all men as brothers, you wipe out one of the most important causes of war, and when you love your neighbor as yourself you wipe out the other, because controversies over religion and commercial rivalry have always been recognized as the two major causes of all war and discord.

Another important result of learning to love God supremely and your neighbor as yourself is not immediately apparent. If you can accept God as Spirit, you can never again fear. You can never fear what form of government we have or any other country has. You can never fear what anyone does. God is then animating human consciousness, and because there is only the power of God, there is nothing left to fear, and when fear is gone, the final cause of our discords is gone.

When we learn to love one another, which means not to fear one another, we have set the pattern for individual and world harmony. We could all live in eternal harmony if we did not fear, but just let fear creep into any group of people and there can easily be a first-class war, and then there would be sides taken: your side and my side. But as long as there is a realization of God as Spirit, no one has anything to fear, for Spirit fills all space, and where the Spirit of the Lord is, there is nothing to fear: no danger, no insecurity, no powers apart from God. Therefore, just to realize that God is Spirit begins to free this whole universe of fear.

Across the Desk

Much of the world belief about God is the truth about the karmic law of cause and effect. It is this general misconception that makes ineffectual so much prayer. Prayer is answered *only* as we come to "know Him aright."

Do you really grasp the significance of *law* and *Grace?* Do you actually discern that God is not responsible for the rewards and punishments we experience? Can you realize that we ourselves set in motion the evil and good influences that touch our lives by our ignorance or by our awareness of the nature of God? Do you understand how the belief in two powers binds us, and how we can release ourselves from the law of cause and effect, at least in a measure, and come under Grace?

Our students should feel a deep sense of responsibility to continue daily specific work for the realization of spiritual government universally expressed. We need to feel God's government as a universal law of peace, justice, life, and love—not that mortals can express these qualities, but that God expresses them as individual being.

~ 4 ~

THE ESOTERIC MEANING
OF THE EASTER WEEK

As we learn to see the significance behind the observance of particular holidays or, more correctly, holy days, we are then able to realize how and why certain days have been set aside by various religious groups as a time for prayer and meditation. Then we can contemplate the principles which these days commemorate rather than consider them as merely holidays from daily work, which often find us no better off the day after than the day before, except for that short period of rest.

When the events which we memorialize as holidays occurred, there undoubtedly was no thought in anyone's mind that because of the happenings of that day, people in far-off places throughout the world would pause in commemoration, but the fact is that these days have become important because the events commemorated illustrate spiritual principles of life which have evolved: principles which all men and women can adopt and by which they can live.

The Humility and Benevolence of Maundy Thursday

The day before Good Friday, Maundy Thursday, Jesus washed the feet of the disciples. He made himself humble before them:

He riseth from supper, and laid aside his garments; and took a towel, and girded himself.

After that he poureth water into a basin, and began to wash the disciples' feet, and to wipe them with the towel wherewith he was girded.

If I then, your Lord and Master, have washed your feet; ye also ought to wash one another's feet.[1]

He fed them at the Last Supper with the bread of life:

Jesus took bread, and blessed it, and brake it, and gave it to the disciples. . . .[2]

He thereby exemplified two of the greatest principles of spiritual living: humility and benevolence, neither of which is correctly understood in human life.

Most persons interpret humility to mean that a person belittles himself or considers himself less worthy than another or beneath someone else. But the true humility of Maundy Thursday, as applied to spiritual living, has no such meaning. True humility is the acknowledgment that I of my own self am nothing: The Father within me is all. It has nothing to do with my being less than you, or your being less than I. It has nothing to do with my holding myself in the background and pushing you into the foreground, or vice versa. It is purely a relationship between God and me. It is an acknowledgment every day and in every way:

I of mine own self am nothing; I of mine own self can do nothing. If I speak of myself, I bear witness to a lie. The Father is the life of my being. The Father within me, the divine Presence ever with me, constitutes my wisdom, intelligence, and sagacity, my strength, my health, and my beauty.

Whatever it is that I may claim as a quality is not mine at all: It is the activity of a spiritual Presence, which functions as I. It created me as an individual entity in the beginning; It formed for me this body, this mind, and this life; and It functions as my intelligence; It functions as my relationships with everyone on earth.

We are only humble in the degree that we actually know that this is true and realize that He that is within us is greater than he that is in the world, or that He performeth that which is given us to do. This is being humble; this is true humility. The only correct self-effacement there is, is the effacement of a personal sense of virtue and the acknowledgment that God has made or given us all that we are, and that God is functioning in us, and through us.

Of old, the purpose of Maundy Thursday was that there might be a complete day of rest for contemplation and meditation on humility and benevolence. Humility must come first because, without it, there can be no truly spiritual sense of benevolence. Always let us remember that in true humility we are not making ourselves lower than someone else: we are subjecting ourselves unto God; we are surrendering ourselves unto God; we are giving to God our mind, soul, spirit, and body, and are acknowledging:

Thou art the life; Thou art the way and the truth. Thou art my being, my wisdom, my guidance, my direction, my support, my supply, my maintenance, and my eternality.

When we begin to understand benevolence in its true light, we shall know that we have never been charitable or benevolent, nor have we ever given anything to anyone—that is, anything that was really ours. We shall understand that whatever it is that we have is ours by the grace of God, and whatever we give, share, or bestow, we do also by the grace of God. We are but the instruments through which God functions, first, to provide us with the twelve baskets full that are left over so that we may share, and then to give us His grace in the form of a will and a desire and an opportunity to share.

There have been persons who have been so generous in their giving that they have impoverished themselves, but that is only because they believed that they were giving of their own possessions and did not understand that they had nothing of their own to give, but that all they apparently possessed belonged to God. It is, for example, like presenting someone with a bouquet of flowers and believing that they are ours. They never were, never are, and never could be: they are God's, formed by God. They were created by God and they grow in our garden by virtue of God. The more we cut and give away, the more we have. They are not our personal possession: they are entrusted to us as an expression of beauty, but we know right well that, if we leave them in our garden, they will only rot and fade away, and certainly not make room for more to grow. It is in the cutting of them, the giving and sharing of them, and in the pruning that we make room for more to grow.

Through the contemplation of Maundy Thursday, we shall learn that, no matter how much of this world's goods we have, these things of the world are not ours. "The earth is the Lord's, and the fulness thereof,"[3] and we can be just as generous with it as we want to be, as long as we recognize, "This that I have is mine by the grace of God, and it is mine to use and to share."

In that attitude, we are impersonalizing good and again we are being humble. Again we are saying, "I am not charitable because I am not giving anything of my own. I am not sacrificing. I am an instrument of God, helping to meet someone else's need: God meeting another's need through me."

"The earth is the Lord's, and the fulness thereof" is not just a scriptural statement of truth: It is a living truth. "The earth is the Lord's, and the fulness thereof," and by the grace of God whatever we possess comes to us, and by the grace of God, also, are we given the desire, the will, and the opportunity to share.

Good Friday: The Crucifixion of Personal Sense

Another holy day of the Easter week is Good Friday. Spiritually speaking, we do not celebrate the crucifixion of the physical form of Jesus. The lesson for us in the crucifixion of Jesus and in his resurrection on the third day is to show us the way to find life eternal. That way, the Master clearly revealed, is by means of the death of personal sense. To be resurrected from the tomb, we must *die* to our personal sense of life, because our personal sense of life is a tomb in which we lie buried. We must *die* to the belief that of our own limited selves we are something, that we have lives of our own, a mind, a soul, a way, and a will of our own. We are to *die* to the belief that we have possessions of our own, or any virtue, any life, any being, any harmony, or any success of our own.

Good Friday is a day in which we should contemplate and meditate upon the inner meaning of crucifixion. By going back to the Gospels, looking upon the Master as a symbol, a way-shower, and reconstructing in our thought his life, ministry, crucifixion, and his resurrection, we can learn how he brought about the death of personal sense, how he avoided being overwhelmed by his problems, even when he had the serious problem of being faced with betrayal and death, and how, by refusing to consider his personal afflictions as problems, he was able to rise above all material sense in the glorious affirmation made when he stood before Pilate: "To this end was I born, and for this cause came I into the world."[4] To him, neither life nor death was a problem.

When Jesus seemed to be in lack at the well of Samaria, and the disciples were concerned with bringing him meat, we note that he says, "I have meat to eat that ye know not of "[5]; and to the woman at the well, "Whosoever drinketh of this water shall thirst again: But whosoever drinketh of the water that I shall give him shall never thirst; but the water that I shall give him shall be in him a well of water springing up into everlasting life."[6]

As we ponder these statements, as well as all the other teachings of Jesus in the Gospels, we come to the realization that what this man is saying in substance is, "I have nothing, but I have everything. I have not where to lay my head, but I have food with which to feed five thousand and twelve baskets full left over." He had meat the world knew not of; he had water that sprang up into life eternal.

This man is a monumental figure. He really had everything: He had God, the Father within, and because he had God, he could share infinity with everyone who lacked, whether it was water or wine, bread or meat, or at the final breakfast, fish. It made no difference what it was: he had it to share, yet he always reminded us that of his own self he could do nothing: "If I bear witness of myself, my witness is not true.[7] . . .Why callest thou me good?"[8]

There we see the principle of Good Friday, the principle of the crucifixion of personal sense, a crucifixion of the belief that we of ourselves have qualities of good or quantities of good. But with that crucifixion, comes the resurrection in the realization, "I am nothing, but I can give you all." Why? Because "the Father that dwelleth in me, he doeth the works."[9]

Instead of thinking of Good Friday as another holy day to be commemorated, what we should realize is that here is a day for the contemplation of another spiritual principle of life: the principle of self-abnegation, in which, when we have brought to light the nothingness of our human selfhood, then is revealed the allness, immortality, and eternality of our being because I and the Father are one, and all that the Father has is mine.

Easter: The Rising Above All Material Ties

That brings us to the Resurrection when, after having died to personal sense and having entombed that false sense of self, our true Self rises out of that tomb of the little self and walks this earth free: free and infinite, immortal and eternal, full of God-being. That is our Easter, our day of ascension, and we find that in our self-renunciation, as in our humility, we have stepped out of a tomb. We are walking the earth now, not full of personal possessions or personal virtues, but filled with the Holy Ghost, the Spirit of the Lord God Almighty which is upon us, and then, we are ordained. Now that material sense has been thoroughly quenched, our real nature, our real being, can come to light.

Paul envisioned this when he revealed to us the two men that we are, each one of us a dual being. We were born the man of earth, and that is what we remain until the crucifixion. That is what we remain as long as we are in the business of glorifying and building up self. But Paul tells us of that other Self which we are, that man who has his being in Christ, that spiritual man or divine Self. That is the man you and I are when we can say, "I can do all things through Christ."[10] Those are the magic words: "I can do all things through Christ, through the Spirit of God in me, through the presence of the Father within me."

Such a person is no more the man of earth. He is no more the man who claims that he is wise, holy, or spiritual. No, that man has been thoroughly crucified, and now we behold a man who recognizes, "By the grace of God, I can do anything—I can do all things through Christ."

Saul of Tarsus was thoroughly crucified. He not only went blind on the road to Damascus; he "died." And out of that tomb stepped Paul, no longer Saul of Tarsus, but Paul: Paul, a man who had his being in Christ and who now lived by the grace of God, a man who traveled not only the Holy Lands, but Rome and Greece, wherever he would, by the grace of God, a man who set up seven churches and found that those seven churches could not support him or his missionary work, but they, looking to him, found that he could support all seven churches.

By virtue of what? He had no gold mines or oil wells, but he had the grace of God; he had his being in Christ; he knew that "I live; yet not I, but Christ liveth in me."[11]

Therefore, he could relax and let this spirit of divine sonship be his bread, his meat, wine, water, and his resurrection and life eternal. When the transition has been made from that man of earth to that man who has his being in Christ, then we find the readiness for the ascension, the ascension which is a rising above every material tie.

There is an indication of that in the passage that is in the beginning of every Infinite Way book and booklet: "Illumination dissolves all material ties and binds men together with the golden chains of spiritual understanding." We do not have to be blood brothers and blood sisters; we do not even have to be brothers or sisters through nationality, or religious brothers and sisters, for we have a holier tie than any human relationship that has ever been conceived. There is a spiritual tie that unites us because we have risen above the belief that we have to be members of one particular human family, racial, religious, or national, in order to be united in a fellowship of love and understanding.

For many years in the Infinite Way we have demonstrated that spiritually we really are of one household. All of you who have been a part of this work since the early days and in the years that have followed have seen in actual practice the most beautiful relationship that can be manifested on this earth, and that without a single tie of human relationship.

With this in mind, do you not see that in the ascension we break every material law and find that man has his being in Christ? The spiritual son is fed from that same spiritual source from which our relationship has been fed and which has maintained us in this relationship through these years. There is no limit to the spiritual demonstration that we can make, except such limitation as we bring upon ourselves by not thoroughly crucifying that personal sense of self.

The Esoteric Meaning of Exoteric Teachings

A spiritual teaching penetrates beneath every human symbol to its spiritual meaning. So whether it is a holiday or holy day, whether it is a relationship, a business, or a government, behind every one of these activities there is a spiritual principle involved, and when that principle is understood and applied in daily life, we are living the mystical or spiritual life, the life that the Master showed us how to live.

Jesus had no hesitancy in urging his disciples to take no thought for what they should eat or what they should drink.

He hesitated not one bit in telling his disciples to set forth on their journey without purse or scrip. From the human standpoint he was not at all practical, yet he is our way-shower and, strangely enough, we shall find if we obey his teachings, that it is very practical to go without purse and without scrip and without taking thought for how anything will be met, because there is an Infinite Invisible. Jesus called It the Father within; Paul called It the Christ, that Something which is and becomes tangibly visible as the bread, water, and wine, the safety, security, and the peace. Spiritual teachings go far beyond merely assuring us of food and clothing and housing.

If we were to consider the subject of safety and security, we would immediately, in all probability, begin thinking in terms of some tangible kind of protection, which might take the form of a bombproof shelter, a bulletproof vest, or a gas mask. Yet these are not necessary, although at times they may be provided, even though no one has to take thought for them or be concerned about them because Scripture reveals that God is a fortress, a high tower, a hiding place, and an abiding place. God is a rock.

When we begin to understand this from a spiritual standpoint, we shall know that it is literally true: not that God provides a rock or a high tower, or a fortress, but that God is Himself the safety, and therefore, those who live and move and have their being in God need take no thought for any material form of protection. This is important to every one of us because from every side there are threatening dangers: infection, contagion, accident, wars, bombs, and a thousand other things. But none of these can come nigh our dwelling place, if our thought is not on physical safety and security, but is held steadfastly to the realization of God as the temple in which we live, the hiding place, the fortress, and the rock.

This is the esoteric meaning of exoteric teaching. In other words, what is plainly set forth for all to read in the scriptures of all peoples of the world are *exoteric* teachings, but each one of these has an *esoteric* meaning, that is, the outer teachings all have inner or hidden meanings. For example, to go through the ritual of a communion service may provide a measure of satisfaction to many communicants, but this is not the real importance of that ritual. The experience of communion takes place within one's Self when the true meaning of being fed the bread or the wine of communion is realized and understood. The real communion is the understanding of the meaning of being fed spiritually, of being fed by *I: I* am the bread of life; *I* am the water; *I* am the blood; *I* am the resurrection; *I* am life eternal. When we understand that, then either the outer communion takes on greater meaning, or it becomes meaningless because now we have that which is greater than the outer form: we have the inner realization.

As you read Scripture, do not read page after page. Read only a small portion at a time, whether the passage is one sentence or whether it is an entire story, such as the experience of Elijah being fed in the wilderness, or Moses' experience in leading the Hebrews out of slavery and carrying them through the wilderness, or some one or another particular phase of Jesus' ministry. Then meditate and contemplate, asking for inner light on the esoteric meaning of those passages. Only trust, and it will be given to you.

To illustrate that point, I recall the many, many years that I could not understand the 91st Psalm. It did not make sense to me when it promised that none of these things would come nigh my dwelling place because they did come nigh my dwelling place, and what is more, I saw them come nigh the dwelling place of all my friends and relatives, too, as well as all the other people that I met in the world. When the time came that I understood all Scripture as having an inner meaning, I prayed, "What is the inner meaning of this much loved Psalm? What does it mean?"

Then one day, as if in great big electric lights, the first verse stood out: "He that *dwelleth* in the secret place of the most High shall abide under the shadow of the Almighty."[12] It does not promise immunity to everybody. It promises immunity to those that dwell "in the secret place of the most High." No one is safe from the snare or from the pit until inwardly he can make this agreement:

I am not living in a material world of time and space. I live and move and have my being in God: I am that man who has his being in Christ. I live with God; I walk with God; I hold my mind steadfast in God; I acknowledge Him in all my ways. In quietness and in confidence, I rest in the assurance of God's presence: God in me, and I in God.

With that in your mind, day in and day out, you are abiding in the Word and letting the Word abide in you, and you will bear fruit richly. No one has the right to feel safe or secure in this world, unless he is living in that Word and letting that Word abide in him, unless he is living and moving and having his being in God-realization, acknowledging God in all his ways, in short, unless he is releasing his life into God.

Do you see why the Master said, "Strait is the gate, and narrow is the way, which leadeth unto life, and few there be that find it"[13]? The world hopes that by going to church on Sunday it can enter into God's grace, but Scripture is very clear about that when it reminds us, "Thou wilt keep him in perfect peace, whose mind is stayed on thee.[14] . . . In all thy ways acknowledge him, and he shall direct thy paths.[15] . . . Abide in me, and I in you."[16] Dwell, live, move, and have your being in the "secret place of the most High." Then you are not of the earth, earthy. Then you are abiding in God, in Spirit where the human mind and its activities cannot reach you, where the laws of matter do not function, and you find yourself free.

You will not, however, find yourself instantly one hundred per cent free. There are still periods of sickness and even periods of lack, or periods of temptation to sin, and maybe even some falling by the wayside and some sinning. Everyone stumbles: some physically, some mentally, some morally, some financially. The sin is not to stumble, but to stumble and never rise again. To pick one's self up after a fall and begin all over again is the spiritual way, a way for which the Master provided when he reminded us to forgive unto seventy times seven. And if we are supposed to forgive seventy times seven, surely the heavenly Father forgives seven thousand times seventy times—without limit.

If overnight you do not find yourself in that land of milk and honey, remember that it took Moses forty years to get there. It took Elijah quite a long time before he found the seven thousand who had not bowed their knees to Baal and who were saved out for him. It took Jesus three years to fulfill his spiritual ministry, and even then he had to encounter actual death before he could experience Resurrection and Ascension.

So do not be surprised or disappointed if you fall down or fail many times. Everyone who has been this way before you has done the same. There are no great spiritual lights who have not come up through trials and tribulations of one sort or another, and probably those who have the greatest love in their hearts, those who have the greatest spiritual gifts of all, are those who have most deeply experienced failure and, therefore, know what it means to walk with us in our failures. Those who have risen highest and can still look down to where they were are the ones who help us the most on the way. Those who do not understand forgiveness do not understand love, and those who do not understand love do not understand the Spirit of the Lord God Almighty.

The Final Step Must Be Taken Alone

The spiritual life is an individual life. There are ways of receiving help from a teacher and from one another, but the final battle and final victory are entirely individual matters, which must be fought out in the consciousness of each one of us. Jesus probably could have received a little support from his disciples in the Garden of Gethsemane; he did not get very much, but the fact that he expected more showed that it was possible. But even if he had, he still had Golgotha, he still had the crucifix, and he still had the tomb. That had to be worked out in his own consciousness.

Only those who have received the light can know what a terrible struggle it is before it comes. Moses was alone on the Mount when he received his light, and it must have been a tremendous struggle before it broke through. He had to be alone to struggle out of his humanhood into the realization of his divine nature and mission. Remember how Moses even refused the mission, how he felt himself unworthy and ill-prepared, and that, too, he had to fight out within himself until he could come to the realization that this was not his message or his mission: It was God's, and he would let God use his body; God would have to talk for him, and through him.

Everyone who attains, attains for himself, within himself. All such are fortunate if they find a teacher who can be a help to them for a time; they are fortunate if they find companions on the way with whom they can share many hours, many experiences, and who can help.

But always remember that the final demonstration you make alone. Jesus made it without mother, without father, without sister, without brother, even though in the end they all came back to him.

As trials and tribulations come, you are both wise and fortunate if you have a teacher to whom you can go and from whom you can receive your help. You are blessed if you have even one person with whom you can walk, with whom you can share—whom you can help and from whom you can receive help.

But never forget this: You cannot enter the kingdom of God two by two. All alone, you take that last mile. All alone, you receive your illumination. All alone, you receive your particular temptation in the form of disease, accident, sin, death, poverty, or lonesomeness—all alone. You resolve all temptations within yourself. You struggle with them inside your own being, just as a mother has to struggle out her life with her child or her children. Nobody can do that for a mother; nobody can relieve her of the responsibility; nobody can perform the function of a mother for her. Every mother has to break her own heart over her own children, and even a husband has to stand by and watch.

So it is on the spiritual path. No one can take your temptation from you but you, and no one else can surmount the temptation. No one can spend the hours of meditation for you; no one can put in the hours of study for you; and no one can be alone with you in your inner sanctuary in those hours preceding illumination. That is why this path is a difficult one. You have to take Scripture and pray for guidance on every passage that contains a principle or spiritual law, and let its esoteric meaning come forth from within yourself.

Maundy Thursday, Good Friday, and Easter Sunday: these are all symbolic of stages in our spiritual on-going. You will have to struggle every single day to remind yourself that every quality, every thought, and every thing that you possess are yours only by the grace of God, but because they are yours by the grace of God, you can share liberally. This, you have to bring consciously to your remembrance; no one can do it for you. You must do it, and one day—it may be weeks or it may be months later—if it is faithfully performed, one day all of a sudden, it comes, and you know, "Whereas before I was blind, now I understand. It is really true: all that I am, I am by the grace of God." Personal sense is crucified, and the resurrected Self, no longer earthbound, rises to the heights of spiritual realization.

Across the Desk

Every day, give sufficient time to a contemplative meditation embodying our major principles of healing. Realize that our goal is the conscious awareness of the spiritual Presence, the attainment of *"My*** peace," the remembrance of *Thy* grace as our sufficiency. Understand that He is closer than breathing and that He performeth that which is given us to do. Feel within yourself that the invisible Spirit goes before you, that It never leaves you nor forsakes you. Acknowledge that in every phase of your daily life there is a divine law and life governing your every activity.

In this contemplative meditation, give God the first-fruits of your day, give Him love and gratitude, give

---

*The word "My," italicized, refers to God.

Him recognition and joy. Then realize that His grace is present with men everywhere, to bless, forgive, establish, and re-establish. Finally, ponder the meaning of Omnipotence, Omnipresence, and Omniscience.

In this same contemplative meditation, look at the evils that appear in "this world" and, regardless of how many appear or what forms they assume, impersonalize them by your understanding that these are the mesmeric pictures of sense, pictures of the carnal mind or the belief in two powers. Since these are not ordained of God and have no law of God to sustain them, they dissolve of their own nothingness. Only that which is of God has law and life. All else is illusion. Understand that since God is one, there is but one power; and therefore, there are no powers to overcome or destroy. "Resist not evil" because you understand the illusory nature of appearances.

Remember that in prayer the words themselves count for nothing: it is the understanding and feeling behind the words that constitute the power. Finally, realize that the function of the Christ is to break the attachment to "this world"–not to increase the things of this world. This is the way whereby reality is attained, freedom from concern about appearances, and freedom to live.

Now we are attuned and prepared to hear His word. Now we are ready to enter His kingdom.

Be at peace. *My* Spirit comforts and prospers you. *My* grace is thy fulfillment.

~ 5 ~

Steps on the Path of Illumination

The goal of our work is the attainment of some measure of spiritual consciousness: to return to the Father's house and thereby attain some degree of that spiritual light which will result in our again becoming children of God. The human race, as we know it, is not the offspring of God. It would dishonor God to believe that He could create what confronts us as human beings; it would be a travesty on God to believe that the conditions existing in this world today were created by Him.

The Master's message was very clearly one of *dying daily* in order to be reborn of the Spirit. Paul, too, made it clear that as creatures we are not under the law of God, "neither indeed can be," but that we can become children of God, we can return to the Father's house and once again be under the law of God, the protection and care of God. The Master's entire mission was to reveal how the transition from the man of earth to that man who has his being in Christ can be made; his entire mission was to reveal the nature of spiritual revelation, spiritual realization, spiritual attainment.

Most of the great religious teachings of the world have adopted as their theme the idea that the man of Adam is outside the Garden of Eden, that is, outside the kingdom of God, and that through spiritual living, practice, and prayer, he can be returned to the Kingdom and again come under the grace of God. This process is known as illumination. Those who are illumined are those who have risen above mortal or material consciousness, those who have received light and, in some cases, initiation.

Gaining Freedom from Material and Mental Laws

There have been brotherhoods, mystical orders, many of which operated on the principle that the initiate could be prepared by degrees for further light, taken from one stage into another and another until eventually illumination took place, resulting in a transcending of material consciousness into a measure of consciousness whereby the individual came under spiritual law.

As human beings, we are under the laws of matter and mind, but these laws of matter and of mind are not laws of God. The reason we know that these laws are not laws of God is because laws of matter or of mind can be, and are, used for good or for evil, but the laws of God cannot be used at all. No one has ever been able to use a law of God: one can be used by the law of God; he can be a servant of the law of God; he can be an instrument through which God works, but he cannot *use* God.

As children of God, we are used *by* God and by God's laws, and are governed by those laws; but God does not know good and evil because, in the realm of God, there are no pairs of opposites. In the realm of God there is neither health nor disease; there is neither youth nor age; there is neither life nor death: there is just a continuity of immortal being.

God changes not; God is the same from everlasting to everlasting, and His ways are perfect. "In him is no darkness at all"[1]—in Him there is no evil; in Him there is nothing of a negative nature: there is only the perfection and immortality of eternal and infinite being. The person who rises even slightly into spiritual realization becomes in a small degree free of material and mental powers, a freedom noticeable in life even if only in a measure.

In the earliest stages of spiritual attainment, we do not immediately embody our full and complete spiritual freedom, nor do we at once gain immunity from all the laws and powers of matter and mind; but in proportion to our attainment of spiritual light do material and mental powers lessen their hold upon us, and we then become less the victims of the changing good and evil of the material sense of life. Not only do we become less victims of material and mental laws, but we also lose the capacity to use material or mental laws in our relation-ships with one another.

In the less evolved stages of human life, it seems normal and natural to accept the eye-for-an-eye-and-a-tooth-for-a-tooth law or to take up swords, even legal swords, against one another; but those men and women who are in the world but not of it and who have attained some measure of spiritual light resort less and less to the use of material, legal, or even mental weapons. There is a gradual surrender of what we call our rights, and a greater degree of reliance on God's ability to establish our rights for us, within us, and through us.

The entire human picture changes for those on the spiritual path, and they do not come under material laws to the extent that they formerly did. Furthermore, as students of spiritual wisdom they are less subject to the laws of disease than they were before they began to pursue this study.

If we were to trace the history of the families who have lived for years with metaphysical or mystical religious teachings as their guide, we would soon discover how comparatively little disease, lack, poverty, and inharmony have been their lot. This does not mean that they have yet attained complete freedom, but only that even a degree of spiritual freedom includes a freedom from the discords of the flesh and that the ultimate and perfect freedom is proportionate to spiritual growth.

Attaining the Transcendental Consciousness

In order to attain some measure of this spiritual Consciousness, it is necessary that specific principles be followed. This message, therefore, contains certain principles which, when read, studied, practiced, and embodied in consciousness, become operative as the fourth dimensional or transcendental Consciousness, a consciousness which is attained in one of two ways.

The first way of attaining this Consciousness is by an act of God, which sometimes takes place in the experience of an individual and, for some unknown reason and without any effort on his part, lifts him into this fourth dimensional or transcendental Consciousness. This is the gift of God.

In this chapter, we are going to deal primarily with the second way which is a conscious attainment of this higher Consciousness.

In our human state, we have been taught to rely almost entirely on our human wisdom, our physical strength, or our personal efforts. The object of turning to a spiritual teaching is to enable us to release ourselves from the strain of modern day life to living "not by might, nor by power, but by my spirit,"[2] to letting the Christ live our life. Grace then begins to take over, and our life is lived more by It and less by personal effort.

There is an invisible Presence that goes before us to "make the crooked places straight,"[3] that goes before us to prepare a place for us; there is a Presence that acts as an intuitive sense, leading us in the right direction. The goal of spiritual living is the attainment of that Consciousness.

Put Up Thy Sword

As human beings, we live by power; most of us rely on material or mental power of some kind. It may be a stronger form of material power overcoming a lesser form of material power, or it may be a mental power overcoming a material force, but the entire human experience consists of overcoming one power by the use of a higher or stronger power. In the metaphysical world, the forces of matter are overcome by the forces of mind, resulting in mind over matter and even mind over mind.

On the path of the Fourth Dimension, however, that is done away with because in the Fourth Dimension, there is no power. Here we make use of no power; here we enter the realm revealed by the Master: the resist-not-evil realm, the put-up-thy-sword realm. Here we learn to relax and put up our mental sword, and when we are tempted with a material or a mental power, threatening our comfort, health, well-being, safety, or security, we do not deny or affirm: instead we release ourselves from any resistance to that which is appearing to us as evil in any form.

It is not easy to do this because our whole inclination as human beings is to strike out to defend ourselves, and even, where necessary, to take the offensive. It is claimed that through the power of smell, animals can detect fear in human beings and that when they attack a person, they are not attacking him, but are attacking that fear because they realize that that fear could make a person destructive and harmful to them, and therefore they take the offensive and try to destroy him before he can destroy them. A somewhat parallel situation may be noted in the way some persons meet the conditions of human life.

On the other hand, those who have attained some measure of Christ-realization come to the point where they do not rise in righteous rebellion against evil, nor take the offensive against it, nor even put themselves on the defensive, but where they stand still as the Master did before Pilate in the realization: "Thou couldest have no power at all against me, except it were given thee from above,"[4] and there is no need for fear.

In the human scene, it may be perfectly normal and natural to resort to "an eye for an eye, and a tooth for a tooth"[5]; it may be quite legitimate to sue those who would sue us, or to stage a war against a neighboring country. This, however, not only is not right in the spiritual realm, but unnecessary because the evils of this world are evil only in the consciousness that accepts them as such. Wherever there is an acceptance of the universal belief in two powers, there are two powers; and there, two powers operate. Wherever a person rises in spiritual consciousness to a place where he recognizes that the Omnipotence of God—and I now give you that word *Omnipotence* to ponder—makes any other so-called power no power, he discovers that there cannot be Omnipotence *and* another power, there cannot be All-power *and* another power. He either deals with Omnipotence as Omnipotence by being convinced of the nonpower of any other appearance or condition, or he merely pays lip service to it and then sings hymns to God Almighty, but "pass the ammunition."

At any moment that a problem of any nature begins to come to your attention, instantly remember that you are not to take up the sword—not the mental sword or the physical sword—but that you are to relax and resist not evil in the realization of Omnipotence. The next three or four days of your life may be very miserable because when you begin a work of this kind, it seems, as in the case of Jesus when he began his ministry and the devil jumped up at him with three temptations, that two or three devils manage to find you, and each of them has two or three temptations for you. So the first few days may be really rugged.

Often you may have to say, " 'Get thee behind me, Satan.'[6] I am not taking up the sword; I am not resisting or refuting: I am standing fast in Omnipotence, standing fast in the realization that there cannot be two powers if Omnipotence is the truth." Then it may be that the problem becomes more insistent, although in one or two instances the problem may disappear. Do not be too heartened, however, if it does, because you will still have those days ahead when a problem of your own or your family, or a headline in a newspaper, will tempt you to accept a destructive power in the world, an evil force or an erroneous condition, and you will be called upon specifically and concretely to bring to conscious remembrance once again the word *Omnipotence,* All-power, one

Power—not one power over another power because there are not two powers in the spiritual kingdom, one to be used against another. There is only one Power, and the secret of harmonious living is the acknowledgment and recognition of one Power.

The one great failing of the religious world has been believing that God was a great power, sometimes even great enough to heal disease or stop wars, depressions, and panics. Five thousand years of history should have proved to us that God is not such a power. God does not stop wars: this is brought about when the enemy runs out of ammunition. God does not heal disease: either some form of *materia medica* does this, or some spiritually endowed individual who has come to the realization of Omnipotence and therefore can look upon disease as the "arm of flesh" or nonpower. Always remember that we are not dealing with a great power or a power supreme over other powers: we are dealing with an individual acknowledgment; we are standing fast in one Power, besides which there are no other powers.

David and Goliath

The story of David and Goliath illustrates the power of the powerless, that power which to our sense is not power. Goliath is represented as a giant, not only a physical giant, but one clad in an impregnable armor which no power could penetrate. Nothing could reach him; nothing could harm him; and nothing could destroy him because he was so well armed that he was invincible and undefeatable by any weapon that up to that time had been conceived or formed. But what happened to this invincibility? A little mite of a fellow came along with a few stones, and just one of those tiny little stones ended the career of this mighty giant clothed in heavy armor. Could anything be more fantastic than the thought of a little stone leveling a giant, and a well-protected giant at that?

This incident of David's encounter with Goliath contains within it a magical secret. David said, "I come to thee in the name of the Lord of hosts."[7] That is the mystery; that is the miracle; that is the magic; that is the secret! What he really was saying was, "I do not come to you with physical power. I do not come to you with physical might. I have not come with a weapon stronger than the one you have fashioned. No, I have come to you with no weapon at all: I come in the name of God." When the disciples came to the Master so proud and happy that they had been given power over the devil—"even the devils are subject unto us through thy name"[8]—they were rebuked, "Rejoice not, that the spirits are subject unto you; but rather rejoice, because your names are written in heaven."[9] What did he mean when he told them not to rejoice that the devils were subject unto them? Simply that there was no power to be subject unto them! There is no power to be subject unto you. You are living in the name and nature of God, and in that name and nature there is no other power. That is why there is no weapon formed against you that can prosper: not because you have any defense, not because you have any weapon over evil, but because you stand in the name and nature of God.

Were you to admit that any person or influence on earth could be destructive to you in any way, shape, manner, or form, you would most certainly have to find some form of defense against it, some form of power to use against it. But you have the mightiest defense of all: the realization that there is no destructive influence unless God be the destructive influence to any concept unlike Itself. The God-power, the God-realization in you, reveals that nothing in the world of effect, nothing in the world of concepts, nothing in the world of persons is power for good or for evil; and, therefore, you need nothing with which to overcome it.

Watch how this operates in your life as some threat comes to you from some individual or thing. Stand fast in your nature—in the name and nature of God—realizing that no weapon that is formed, no concept that is formed, has power over the truth of being.

This same principle applies in the healing work. If you have accepted the belief of infectious and contagious diseases, inherited diseases, or any other form of disease, watch what happens when you give up your mental weapons and stop fighting it. Watch what happens when you stand in the name and nature of God. There is no weapon, there is no belief, there is no concept of man that can stand in opposition to the name and nature of God.

"The battle is the Lord's"[10]—not yours or mine. We need no physical powers; we need no mental powers: That which is the least of them, a little stone, is sufficient to the tearing down of the stronghold of the mighty Goliath—even a tiny little bit of a stone, nothingness. That which to the world represents no power at all, a little stone, overthrows the mightiest of powers, whether that power is physical or mental.

Spiritual power is self-maintained, a self-created and a self-sustained power, and you have only to let yourself be clothed with this spiritual armor of truth and then to stand in its name and nature. The spiritual armor of truth is not a weapon to be used against error: The spiritual armor of truth is the realization of Omnipotence, that creative Influence which not only created this universe, but which maintains and sustains Itself unto eternity.

If you acknowledge that you are some self other than the divine, you wither. You have then set up that which has to surround itself with armor plate. But when you acknowledge God as your Self, then let God be Its own defense and use no physical or mental weapons. Human weapons are necessary for those on the level of consciousness that live by might and by power, but those who come to that higher level of life by the Spirit cannot use the world's weapons. They learn that God is not a power over other powers. God is a Self-maintained and Self-sustained Power. That is the Power, and that Power is love: not a love that we use for a purpose, but a love which embraces us within Its law and maintains and sustains our being.

Silence and Secrecy

You have to begin this moment to take an attitude in which you accept Omnipotence, God as All, and therefore anything and everything else as the "arm of flesh," temporal power, nothingness. This you must do sacredly and secretly. Do your praying secretly because unless you attain this consciousness within yourself you will never be able to demonstrate it outwardly and openly. Do not go around preaching or teaching this; do not proselyte; do not try to tell your neighbor, your friends, or your relatives how wonderful this is. They would not believe you anyway.

Live this life within yourself until the fruitage of it begins to appear in your experience. Then when you are asked the why and the wherefore of the changes in your life or when you find a receptivity or a sincere interest, you may begin to reveal it, but be sure that you, yourself, are demonstrating it before you begin preaching or teaching it. Do not expect anyone to believe merely what you say because as Emerson said, "What you are . . . thunders so that I cannot hear what you say. . . ." Be assured that no one is going to believe a metaphysical or a mystical cliché simply because you repeat it. Fortunate indeed are you if you find those who believe it after you have demonstrated it.

The Master cautioned us to do our praying secretly, silently, and sacredly, reminding us that "thy Father which seeth in secret himself shall reward thee openly."[11] So I say to you that every step on the mystical path must be a secret one. It is not that we would keep it secret from the world because of a reluctance to share it, but we would keep it secret within ourselves until we have demonstrated it. Then we are more than willing to share it with that part of the world that is led to us.

Always remember that there is a milk of the Word for babes, but there is also a meat of the Word for the mature. Remember not to cast your pearls before swine.

To Whom Much Is Given, of Him Much Is Demanded

In this world, you will continually be faced with the appearance of two powers, and the higher you go in spiritual realization, the more will you be faced with it, because when you have overcome the world for yourself, you will find that you are attracting to you all those who are themselves besieged with the problem of two powers; and so more than ever will you be called upon to stand fast.

If so be an individual ever again rises to the height of Christ Jesus, he will find himself with all the world's problems to be solved. It is for this reason that spiritual attainment is never given to us for our own benefit. Of those who have much, much is demanded; and with every bit of spiritual life that you attain, be assured that you will be called upon to bear more and more witness to it; you will be called upon for more and more service to God. Never believe that the spiritual path leads to sitting in a cave somewhere, hiding away from the world; never believe that it leads to a life of indolence and ease.

"Strait is the gate, and narrow is the way, which leadeth unto life, and few there be that find it,"[12] but when you finally arrive, the work is plentiful. The laborers are few, very few, but the work is world-wide. With every degree of realization you attain, with every bit of confidence you have in Omnipotence, be prepared to be called upon to prove it, over and over again. The time will come when there are no major problems in your own life, and many, many years may go by without your ever being aware of a major problem of your own, but you will be drawing to you those of the world who are seeking the same freedom that you have found, and you will be called upon to work with them—to serve, to heal, and to teach—but only in proportion to your own demonstration.

This is one area in which knowing all the words in all the books will not make you a good teacher. On the contrary, you may know very few words and be the greatest of teachers because the teaching is by demonstration rather than by word of mouth.

The Kingdom of God Realized

To this word *Omnipotence,* let us add another, *Omnipresence,* which is of equal importance. Most people have an idea that God is somewhere up in heaven, in a holy mountain, in a holy temple, or in a holy teacher, but the real truth is that God is closer to you than your very breathing, and nearer than your own hands and feet, and you do not have to go anywhere to find Him. You need only acknowledgment, the recognition of Omnipresence, of God filling all space throughout all time, the recognition that where you are is holy ground.

If you mount up to heaven, you will find God there, and if you make your bed in hell, you will find God there also. When you walk through the "valley of the shadow of death," you will find God there with you, if you have taken that word *Omnipresence* into your consciousness and lived with it. You will be assailed from morning to night with the belief that you cannot reach God, that God is somewhere other than where you are, but now you will be called upon with every one of these temptations to stop your searching, your reaching out for God, and settle back in the realization that where you are God is because of Omnipresence.

Now watch the miracles that begin to take place within a very few days as you learn to relax in the realization of Omnipresence and Omnipotence, as you learn to relax from taking up the sword against some enemy: a physical, mental, moral, or financial one, or against any other mythological beast that walks the earth. Remember that all beasts are mythological because God never made one.

When you have Omnipotence and Omnipresence together in one place at the same time—within your own consciousness—you have the kingdom of God realized within you. The kingdom of God is neither lo here nor lo there; it is not in holy mountains; it is not in holy temples; it is not in holy teachers: "The kingdom of God is within you"[13]; therefore, relax from the strain, relax from striving, and acknowledge Omnipresence, the presence of God where you are:

Neither life nor death can separate me from God. I am in the presence of God, and as long as I am in the presence of God, it matters not whether I am what the world calls alive or dead. I cannot be separated from the life of God, the love of God, the consciousness of God, from the God-being Itself.

Across the Desk

Long ago meditation was discovered and practiced in the Orient, but it became a lost art years before it ever reached the Western world. Now that the secret has been rediscovered, it is being introduced in the West and re-introduced into the East.

The original discoverer of the art of meditation is unknown. He may have been a traveler on the desert who spent his time in contemplating the mysteries of the heavens, one perhaps who knew the stars and some of their secrets; he may have known and contemplated the mysteries of the Sphinx and the pyramids; he may have been a fisherman and known the joy of contemplating the mysteries of the sea, or a shepherd like Moses, contemplating the mysteries of nature, sensing the atmosphere of the mountains and marveling at the fertility of flocks and fields.

Lost in such contemplation, the miracle occurred, the climax of meditation was reached, and an inner release experienced which may have taken the form of a deep breath or sigh, or as of a weight or burden falling from his shoulders. Undoubtedly, there was a sense of inner peace or mild exhilaration, and then a sense of being at peace with all the world.

A continuation of such experiences would eventually result in a complete realization of oneness with all being: with trees and plants, with the birds of the air and the fish of the sea, or it may have lifted him into conscious oneness even with the stars or with the lightning and thunder of a summer storm.

Meanwhile, a great mystery revealed itself to the explorer in this realm of Withinness: he realized that man originally was pure spiritual being, drawing his life, substance, law, and continuity from God, but after the mist arose and man lost his vision of God, he became a lone, lost individual, wandering like the Prodigal, but never reaching home, never reaching his divine consciousness and fulfillment.

Now, through an inner communion with Something greater than himself and an outer communion with every form of life, he was no longer alone or lonesome. The great mystery of Adam was solved: not getting a mate from his rib, but from his heart under the rib, really from that feeling usually attributed to the heart, that feeling of love that wells up in meditation, for it is from this feeling of love within man, which comes only when in contemplation and communion with God, that all the issues of life come forth: companionship, supply, safety, security, peace, joy, health, and completeness.

Contemplating the mysteries of life, its law and beauty, its rhyme and rhythm, its harmonies and moods, led his attention back to his Source, to the realm of the real, the kingdom of God within him, and he experienced the ultimate of meditation in an actual communion with the source and fount of all Being. Then came the release from all care and the solution to all problems, followed by the fulfillment of all good in his experience even without taking thought.

The original wanderer who discovered the secret of life and its harmonious and joyous experience then probably sought out others who were lost on the desert of human existence to whom he might impart the mystery of resurrection from the tomb of mortality, the great secret of the ascension of soul and body to immortal heights. And so the great art of meditation was discovered, taught, and lived.

Somewhat sorrowfully, the teacher of this mystery, like the Master who came later, learned that, whereas he would give his "pearl of great price"[14] to all mankind, like Jerusalem, they "would not."[15] Only the few were receptive, but those few became a people set apart, a joyous people, successful and brilliant because they had all of God upon which to draw for wisdom, light, love, and attainment.

As it became more generally known that these few contemplatives in the world had access to the peace and prosperity of the world, those not spiritually attuned began to look upon meditation as a means of going within solely for the purpose of drawing forth the good things of life: supply, companionship, home, and health.

And so a practice was begun of turning within in an attempt to draw forth *things,* and eventually the art of pure meditation was lost, and meditation became an incomprehensible mystery.

The real mystery of meditation is that meditation is not a means of getting things from the divine center that is within man. Seeking to get, achieve, or attain from the heavenly Kingdom can only result in the loss of the little we already have. Meditation is not a means to an end. Meditation is a contemplation of the deep things of spiritual reality, of the rhythm of the universe, a dwelling in the Kingdom within, and then as its climax an inner communion with the Spirit of man, a contact with his Soul, a revelation of the truth behind the mysteries of life.

The miracle is that without desire, without taking thought, the Presence within goes before to make "the crooked places straight,"[16] to prepare a mansion—many mansions. The divine invisible Presence becomes visible as form—as the very body of all good. A thousand may fall at one's left and ten thousand at the right, but never do the problems of this world intrude into the consciousness of those who live in meditation, in a perpetual inner contemplation, a true communion with the inner Self or Source.

~6~

CONTEMPLATIVE MEDITATION

The entire harmony of your life and the success of the activities of your life depend upon your remembrance and practice of meditation.

A meditation should be directed toward the realization of oneness with God. You should not be thinking of any desired demonstration or of any desired good in your life, of any particular person, circumstance, or condition. Your entire attention should be given to the realization of God, always bearing in mind that the kingdom of God is within you, neither lo here nor lo there, but within you. You will never find it by looking for it in any place other than within your own being.

Once you realize that what you are seeking is within, you will give your entire attention, thought, and activity to that point within you: not within your body, but within your consciousness.

Do not think of any part of your body, of any organ or function of the body: think only of some point within your consciousness and remember that somewhere within you there is a point of contact, a point wherein you and your Father become consciously one. You and your Father are already one, but that relationship of oneness is of no benefit to you until there is a conscious realization of it.

There are far too many students who, because they have been taught that "I and my Father are one"[1] and that they are children of God, believe that this is all that is necessary to bring harmony into their experience. This is not true. There must be an actual contact; there must be an actual experience of oneness. Something must take place within them that brings the assurance that they have realized the Presence.

Let Each Meditation Be an Individual Experience

This awareness of having made a contact may take any number of forms. At times when this contact is made, it is followed by a deep breath, or there may be an awareness of receiving an impression as if some message were being given to you, or there may even be the still small voice that sometimes is audible.

We can never know in what way the realization of God's presence will be made evident to us, and therefore we must never outline how it is to appear or what form it should take. We must never expect to see visions or believe that it is necessary to hear a voice. We must never outline what the experience will be because it can take place in one form today and in another tomorrow; it can appear one day one way and another day another way; but if we are outlining in our mind what should happen, we are trying to mold the experience according to some preconceived idea instead of letting the experience unfold itself to our awareness.

As you meditate, remember that you must have no object, no purpose, no goal, and no desire other than the experience of God-contact or God-realization. You must not have in mind any object that you wish, or any desired demonstration. You must never have in mind the healing of mind, body, lack, or fear. Never, never, must you have any goal or any object other than the attainment of God-realization and the recognition of the Presence within you.

A Contemplative Form of Meditation on God

If you cannot quickly feel at peace with a kind of listening attitude, then you might begin with a meditation in which you contemplate God and the things of God. You might begin with the word God, letting anything come into your thought on the subject of God that wishes to unfold:

God is closer to me than breathing. God is already where I am, for "I and my Father are one,"[2] *and not even life or death can separate me from God.*

God is the very substance of my form. Even my body is the temple of God because God formed it.

God formed this entire temple of the universe: "The earth is the Lord's, and the fulness thereof."[3] *God made it in the image and likeness of His own substance.*

God is really my identity, constituting my individuality. If I am a painter or a musician, God has given me the inspiration and the ability and the skill; if I am a novelist, God has given me the ideas with which I work and the skill to express them; if I am in a business or a profession, God is the intelligence that governs my activity.

As a matter of fact, if I am healthy, it is because God is the health of my countenance. God is my fortress. I live and move and have my being in God, and that is why we are inseparable and indivisible.

God in me is the kingdom of God within me, and in this oneness is that divine relationship of Father and son.

"Son, thou art ever with me, and all that I have is thine."[4]
*My sonship with God entitles me to all that God is and all that
God has, not by virtue of my being good, not by virtue of my
deserving or earning it—because in my human capacity I can
hardly be worthy of God—but because I am the son of God,
because the relationship between God and me is a relationship
of oneness, because God has decreed, "Son, thou art ever with
me, and all that I have is thine." Because of this, God's grace
is mine.*

*God's grace is not something to be earned or won or de-
served; God's grace is not something that takes place in the
future: God's grace is functioning within me now. God's grace
functions to support, maintain, and sustain me. God's grace
functions as my inspiration, my skill, my ability, and my
integrity.*

I have no integrity of my own *of which to boast, no honesty*
of my own, *no morality* of my own—*nothing of which I can
boast—because God constitutes the integrity of my being. God
constitutes my capacity for work, and God constitutes my
capacity for thought and for inspiration. "Son . . . all that I have
is thine"; therefore, God is my all-capacity, my infinite capacity.*

*God constitutes the infinite nature of my supply. My supply
is not limited to my activity, to my knowledge or wisdom, to
what I can earn, or to what anyone can give me. My supply is
limited only to the infinite nature of God's gift: " 'Son, thou art
ever with me, and all that I have is thine': thou art heir, joint
heir, to all that I have." My supply is as infinite as God's
capacity is to bestow.*

*"The earth is the Lord's, and the fulness thereof." All this
earth, the skies and the sun and the moon and the stars, and all
the fish of the sea, and all the birds of the air, all the perfume
of the flowers—all of this is mine because "Son, thou art ever
with me, and all that I have is thine."*

God is closer to me than breathing. God is with me if I mount up to heaven; God is with me if I make my bed in hell; God is with me if "I walk through the valley of the shadow of death." [5] *I need fear no evil for God's presence is with me, and God's presence goes before me to make the crooked places straight. God's presence goes before me to prepare mansions for me; God's presence is the very meat, wine, and water of my daily life; God's presence is the assurance of my infinite supply.*

Because God is my hiding place, God's presence is my protection, my safety, and my security. I find my safety and security within me; I carry it with me in life and in death, because I carry with me the presence of God.

In this meditation, all that you have done is to contemplate God: the presence of God, the allness of God, and your relationship to God. You have dwelt in a continuous contemplation of God's allness, God's mightiness, God's grace, God's love; and having come to the end of your thoughts for the moment, you now become quiet and wait for God to speak to you. You keep silent while your ears are open as if the still small voice were about to speak to you. This voice may speak in actual words; it may come forth merely as an impression or a feeling of God's presence; or it may leave you with nothing more than a deep breath.

In one way or another, however, within the next twenty, thirty, or forty seconds, you will feel It and have a conviction that you are not alone, but that there is a Presence within you. The moment you have gained that awareness, you have made your conscious contact with God and have attained the conscious realization of your oneness with God. Your oneness has always existed, but now you have taken the further and all important step of attaining conscious oneness or a conscious realization of your oneness.

Fulfillment Is Attained by Conscious Oneness

This is when the miracle really begins because in the moment that you attain conscious realization of your oneness with God, you also attain your oneness with all forms of good necessary to your experience. These, then, begin to come to you without taking thought for them. In other words, when you attain conscious oneness with God, you attain oneness with the evidence of your supply; you attain oneness with companionship; you attain oneness with home; you attain oneness with employment, with inspiration, art, literature, or music. You attain oneness with everything necessary to the fulfillment of your life.

The scriptural promise, "In thy presence is fulness of joy; at thy right hand there are pleasures for evermore,"[6] becomes literally true in the experience of every person who attains conscious oneness with God because he then attains his oneness with his rightful companionship, his rightful home, his rightful sense of supply, his rightful business, his rightful artistic, literary, or musical skill. Whatever it is that represents fulfillment in his life is attained by virtue of conscious oneness with God.

It has been demonstrated for thirty years in the experience of our students that as they have attained this conscious realization of their oneness with God, events in the outer world began to change, and either new sources of supply, new sources of activity, or new professions were opened to them. Call it what you will, by whatever name or form, these students have found that fulfillment began to be expressed and eventually there came a sense of true completeness.

In the consciously realized presence of God is the fulfillment of life. You may never have painted a picture in your life, but if you have dreamed of doing so, you may do so now; you may never have had music in your life, but if you have dreamed of it, you will have it as a part of your experience now. In other words, something within changes the outer experience.

As human beings, we live completely cut off from God, exemplifying the Master's statement: "If a man abide not in me, he is cast forth as a branch, and is withered; and men gather them, and cast them into the fire, and they are burned."[7] As human beings we have only our own wisdom and experience, our own physical strength, health, and dollars, and all of these are limited. But the moment that we adopt the teaching of the fifteenth chapter of John of abiding in *Me* and letting *My* words abide in you, then we are as a branch of a tree that is one with the vine, and all that God is, is flowing through that vine into expression through us, and we now have conscious contact with the infinite Storehouse which is the creative, sustaining, and maintaining Power behind this universe.

In spring it is particularly easy to observe the fullness of the beds of grass, the leaves on the trees, the buds and the blossoms, and the abundance of all these. A few months previously there was no green grass, there were no leaves, no buds or blossoms: all was barrenness. Then suddenly there is fullness. How could this happen except through the activity of an invisible Presence and Power which, at the right season of the year, bursts forth into visibility as new grass, new buds, new blossoms, new fruit, and fills all nature with an infinite, beautiful, practical, and useful abundance? And all of this from an invisible Withinness unseen to the human eye.

This same unseen, infinite manufacturing Plant operates in your consciousness. It is invisible, and while you can never become aware of it through your physical senses, you can become aware of the fruitage of it as you begin to see more abundant supply and happier relationships in every area of your life.

When this occurs, you will begin to realize that this is the outer evidence of that invisible Essence, Spirit, or Storehouse which is likewise providing all nature with fulfillment. It is this that fills rivers, lakes, and oceans with fish and the air with birds, but the reason all these forms of life receive their abundance and experience their fulfillment in due season without ever taking thought is because there has been no break in their relationship with the invisible Source.

With man this is different. With man there has been a break, and as a human being, he has no contact with God. He is not under "the law of God, neither indeed can be,"[8] until he restores to himself his original relationship with his Father. Then his life will change just as did that of the Prodigal Son when he returned to his father's house and was given the robe and the ring of divine sonship.

Beginning the Journey Back to the Father's House

When we realize our barrenness, the futility of human life, and how difficult and what a struggle life is physically and mentally, and how little help we seem to be getting from any divine Source, we begin to wonder if there is a God or if there is any way to approach God. Then begins our return journey to our Father's house, a journey that is accomplished within our consciousness, not by going to holy mountains or holy temples or holy teachers. All these may play a part in our lives, but they are not essential.

The first essential is the realization that within us is the kingdom of God and that this Presence and Power must be contacted or found within us. From that point on, we will be led along the way: we may be led to certain books; we may be led to certain teachings or teachers, all of whom can play an important part in our unfoldment. We may eventually find that within us something almost indescribable takes place, and we may become aware that angels are ministering unto us–not the feathered kind, but nonetheless angels, divine inspirations–and that which we recognize as spiritual help of one sort or another. We may find that we are being guided and being led in ways that are entirely foreign to us–ways we never knew existed.

That is because now the son of God is within us, the son of God which is our real identity, our real Selfhood. The outer expression which is called William or Mary or Martha is but the outer seeming sense of the reality which is our invisible Withinness. In other words, in this human sense of life, we are two persons, not one. The Master said: "I and my Father are one.[9] . . . [but] my Father is greater than I"[10]; and Paul said: "I live; yet not I, but Christ liveth in me."[11] They both meant the same thing. They both meant that there is this outer person whom we call Jesus or Paul, or Mary or Martha, but there is also the greater Self which is the real Self, the spiritual identity, the son of God. The moment we make contact with that, we no longer live our own lives, but we find that there is a spiritual Presence, a spiritual Power, a spiritual Guide, always coming through to us provided we give It the opportunity.

Admittedly, it is undoubtedly more difficult to live the spiritual life today than it was many years ago, because never before have there been so many outward distractions to keep us from our periods of inner communion with God. There is a price tag on the life of the Spirit, and the price is the setting aside of sufficient periods in the day and the night for inner communion. This inner communion begins with contemplative meditation, leading eventually to a deeper meditation in which there are no longer statements of a contemplative nature, but there is a communion in which we receive impartations from the depths within us. This is God speaking to us instead of our assuring and re-assuring ourselves.

The contemplative form of meditation is a necessary step for most persons and one that must be used for a long time, until the inner communion is so well established that one can instantly settle into an inner peace and immediately become receptive to the impartations that unfold from within one's own being. This in time leads to a further step in which we go from a communion with God to an actual, realized oneness with God, and in this there are no longer words or thoughts, but only a divine state of Being in which one realizes oneself as the life of all that exists.

Many students of metaphysics have been accustomed to thinking of prayer and treatment as a means of attaining something through God, but in this work of the Infinite Way that is never done. On this path, at no time is truth ever used to gain any end or for the purpose of making any demonstrations; at no time is God considered an instrument whereby to get something. In the Infinite Way, there is no purpose or goal beyond God-realization, and once God-realization has been attained, that realization takes care of everything that happens in life.

In the preceding chapter, the word *Omnipotence* brought forth the idea that if there is Omnipotence or All-power, then there cannot be any other power. With this realization, we instantly lose our fear of material conditions, forces, or powers, and even our fear of mental forces or powers. We rest in the assurance that since there is but one power we have nothing to fear. The so-called evils of the world have no power or presence, and they should not be fought, nor should any attempt be made to be rid of them. They should be recognized as illusory appearances.

Just as the concept of Omnipotence dissolves our fear of other powers and permits us to rest in the assurance of one power, so does the word *Omnipresence* allay our fear of any other presence because, as a matter of fact, there cannot be All-presence *and* another presence. When you grasp the real significance of Omnipotence and Omnipresence, you have set yourself apart from any of the evils of this world, which are instantly recognized as appearance, illusion, or maya—call it what you will.

Omniscience Changes Your Concept of Prayer

What really changes your life, however, is an understanding of Omniscience because this changes your whole concept of prayer. There are fifty centuries of erroneous prayers in our background, fifty centuries of praying amiss. There have been only a few brief years of praying aright in the whole of the last fifty centuries, and therefore, we really have some overcoming to do in order to correct the erroneous sense of prayer into which we were born and under which we have been brought up.

Think of the meaning of Omniscience; look it up in the dictionary and try to get a full and complete understanding of All-wisdom and All-knowledge. Then think of what you have really been doing when you have prayed to God and told God what you need, and sometimes even on what day you needed it. Think of what you have been doing when you have been asking God to heal your child or some dear soul who needs it, as if God were not omniscience. Think of what you have been doing when you pray God to send you supply.

Did not Jesus know what he was talking about when he said: "Your heavenly Father knoweth that ye have need of all these things.[12] . . . for it is your Father's good Pleasure to give you the kingdom"[13]? Did not Jesus know about prayer when he said, "Take no thought for your life, what ye shall eat, or what ye shall drink; nor yet for your body, what ye shall put on"[14]? Are we not violating that teaching when we pray to God for supply, for home, for companionship, for a vacation, or for an automobile? Are we not really paying only lip service to an omniscient God?

The word *Omniscience* reminds us of what we have been doing in our prayers. Have we not been guilty of telling God something? Have we not been reminding God of something? Have we not been asking something of God that we think God does not know anything about? Have we not been telling God of someone who needs Him?

Think what you do when you go to God with anything that you wish to convey to this Omniscience, to this All-wisdom, All-knowledge, All-power, All-presence; and then you will quickly learn how to transform your prayer into a righteous prayer, a prayer that is a resting back in God in an inner assurance that "before they call, I will answer; and while they are yet speaking, I will hear,"[15] that before you know your need He knows it, and it is His "good pleasure to give you the kingdom."[16] Think of how this will change your prayer as you learn to look upon God as the great All-wisdom, All-presence, and All-power.

Suppose that we had to remind God to put apples on apple trees, peaches on peach trees, or berries on berry bushes; or suppose that we had to remind God that we need or do not need so much rain, or remind Him every evening that it should become dark and the stars should come out and the moon. God is doing all these things without our advice or petitions and can we not trust Him enough to know our needs without reminding Him of them?

If God knows enough to continue to put the fish in the sea and the birds in the air, if God knows enough to keep the tides in their places, ebbing and flowing on schedule, if God knows enough to keep this earth and all the other planets in their orbits, surely God knows our need, and if God has the love to supply all the needs of this world, God has enough love to supply us with ours. Only our egotism would interfere with our receiving it, only the egotism that believes we know our need better than God does, only the egotism that believes we have more love for our children than God has for His: only such rank egotism can prevent the free flow of God's grace to us.

Once we have overcome this egotistic sense, we can relax in the realization that God is Omniscience, Omnipresence, and Omnipotence; and we can stop taking thought for our life, for what we shall eat, or what we shall drink. We can stop taking thought and begin to acknowledge God, and as we acknowledge Him in all our ways, keeping our thoughts stayed on Him, we find that God is operating in our experience and that as a need arises it is met usually before we know that the need is there.

So it is that prayer is our point of contact with God; it is through prayer that we establish our conscious oneness with God; it is through prayer that we establish our conscious awareness of God's presence; it is through prayer that we acknowledge that even "though I walk through the valley of the shadow of death, I will fear no evil: for thou art with me"[17]; it is through prayer that we rest in the assurance of God's presence, God's grace, and God's law. Then we relax and find that this invisible Presence does for us exactly what it does for the trees and the grass in their seasons, and for all the rest of this vast universe.

Practicing the Presence

When we are acknowledging God as Omnipotence, Omnipresence, Omniscience, we are practicing the presence of God, keeping our mind stayed on God, and we are setting up within ourselves an inner stillness that later becomes a receptivity to the presence of God,

Itself, to that which has been called the birth of the Christ.

The birth of the Christ is that moment in our individual experience when *nothing* becomes tangibly something, when, where there was a lack of something, all of a sudden there now becomes evident a Presence, tangible and real, a power, a companion, a savior, a guide. From that moment on, we consciously abide in the Presence.

Because of the realized presence of God within us, it would be impossible for there to be any strife with anyone. In the human picture we may disagree, but there could be no conflict of a really harmful or destructive nature between us if even one of us had realized the Presence. As this Presence lives in us, it becomes impossible for us to take up a sword, to hate or envy, be jealous, malicious, or destructive.

The entire secret of peace on earth is the establishing in our consciousness of this realized Presence, which acts as a leveler in our consciousness, making us all equally children of God. This makes it possible to realize what the Master meant when he said, "Call no man your father upon the earth: for one is your Father, which is in heaven"[18]–one creative Principle.

So we learn not to call our country, *our* country, or our flag, *our* flag. We give it its due, but we recognize that we are all of one spiritual household. This does not mean only those on our particular path. It means that every individual on the face of this globe actually has but one Father, one creative Principle, and in our recognition of that we are brothers. The fact that there may be cultural, educational, or economic levels that separate us at the moment has nothing to do with the basic truth that we are equally one insofar as our spiritual relationship is concerned. We all have but one creative Principle, one Father; and some day we shall all begin to act as though we really believed that.

If we are to do that, it will be necessary for us to change our concepts of prayer and begin to treat God as if that omnipotent, omnipresent, and omniscient God really were closer to us than breathing. Our function is to rest in God. But we must never try to bend God to our will or try to get God to do something for us that we want, because we will not succeed. Whenever we are tempted to try to get God to do something, remember that we are trying to bend Him to our will and then we will be released from any such paganistic concept of prayer, and we will pray:

Mold me to Thy will; bend me to Thy will; make me yield myself unto Thy will so that Thy will, and not mine, be done in me. Let me not have a will of my own; let me not have a desire; let me not have a wish: Let me completely yield myself to Omniscience, Omnipotence, and Omnipresence, and be a beholder of what takes place in my life as I permit an All-knowing, All-power, All-presence govern my life.

Across the Desk

Resurrection, in its mystical sense, means resurrecting the Son of God out of the tomb of the physical senses. It is also resurrection in the sense of rising out of the physical sense of body into the realization of spiritual consciousness as governing all form.

The revelation of life lived by Grace instead of under the law consists of the revelation of the consciousness of the individual as a law of resurrection, healing, and protection to the body, business, home, and well-being in every form, and we begin to see how consciousness—the consciousness of the individual—even without taking thought and without being directed, becomes the law of harmony unto our experience.

~7~

THE DICE OF GOD ARE LOADED

During the past one hundred years, the world has learned a great deal about the laws underlying natural phenomena; and because of this increase in knowledge, power heretofore unknown is now being harnessed and utilized. There is another law, however, a far different kind of a law that has been known to the world for thousands of years, although never understood or practiced by any very large segment of the population. If this law could be known and practiced, it would not only set individuals free, but entire communities as well.

There is perhaps no better way to explain this law of life than to quote from Emerson's essay on "Compensation":

> There is always some leveling circumstance that puts down the overbearing. . . . Though no checks to a new evil appear, the checks exist, and will appear. . . . The dice of God are always loaded.

Yes, "the dice of God are always loaded." What a statement! What tremendous significance can be found in those few words!

Think back to Caesar who governed with an iron hand, to Genghis Khan, to Alexander the Great, and as we come to more modern days, think of the Czars of Russia, think of Mussolini, Hitler, and Stalin. Call to mind the all-powerful ones who could not be conquered, who carried everything before them. Think! Go back in history and you will find dozens of other illustrations, and see if you do not agree that "the dice of God are always loaded." Even though at the moment there appears to be nothing to stop the onward march of tyranny, of evil in one form or another, inevitably these checks appear and become manifest.

As Ye Sow

"There is always some leveling circumstance that puts down the overbearing," but Emerson does not state what it is that creates this leveling circumstance. He might have done so, because he knew what it was. It is the law of *as ye sow so shall ye reap:* whatever you do to another, so it shall be done unto you; whatever you bind will bind you, but whatever you set free will set you free. All life flows out from the center of your being, and all outward circumstances are governed and controlled by this inner law.

The law is very clear: "For he that soweth to his flesh shall of the flesh reap corruption; but he that soweth to the Spirit shall of the Spirit reap life everlasting."[1] Of course, the questions inevitably arise: What is meant by sowing to the flesh? What is meant by sowing to the Spirit? And I might answer them by asking another question: Do you place power in flesh or in effect, or do you place power in an invisible Source? For example, as you look at world conditions today, ask yourself if you are fearing the power of men. If you are fearing "man, whose breath is in his nostrils,"[2] you are sowing to the flesh and will reap corruption. On the other hand, if you are placing your faith or confidence in man, or if you have any belief that there is a man or a group of men who can save this world, you are likewise sowing to the flesh because putting faith in princes–"man, whose breath is in his nostrils"–has raised up in the world the greatest betrayers of mankind. Remember that every man who has ever betrayed anyone or anything was able to do so only because he was placed in a position of power by the people themselves, the people whose confidence he had first gained. A person must first be given power before he can betray that power.

Whether we are thinking in terms of national or international affairs or merely our own personal affairs, it all comes down to the fear of what mortal man can do to us, or what effect human circumstances or conditions can have upon us, or what faith we may have that there is a man or group of men who can save us individually or save the world collectively. The effect in either case would be the effect of sowing to the flesh and thereby reaping corruption.

To begin to understand that there is an invisible law operating–the karmic law of *as ye sow so shall ye reap*–and that that law is operating in consciousness would tend to stop one's fears because it immediately gives the assurance that evil, in and of itself, cannot be perpetuated. Evil, in and of itself, cannot stand. The very moment that we withdraw power from idols, the minute we withdraw power from men or organizations and place that power in the Invisible, we automatically and instantly release ourselves from any evil that men or conditions can do to us. This does not mean that we are able to release the world from evil immediately. No, first we release ourselves, and then, in proportion as we are released, do we bring release to those who come within range of our consciousness.

There Is No Power in the Visible

The Bible tells us that ten righteous men can save a city. So, too, a very small group of individuals who no longer place their confidence in a political party or in some political candidate can change the entire results of an election. That does not mean that they necessarily will elect the particular candidate of their chosen party, but it does mean that those candidates nearest to the level of spiritual integrity will be elected. This would come about only as those who are able to give up their faith and confidence in any man or party realize that there is no power in the visible.

Let me put it this way: In certain areas, votes are controlled by certain interests. For example, in some communities it is believed, and the results would seem to bear it out, that the labor vote controls the election; in some other community, because the majority of the citizens belong to a certain church it is believed that that will be the decisive factor in the election; in some other area, the industrialists apparently control the votes. It is this very belief that perpetuates the evils of our political life; but actually, the power is not in a ruthless individual or in some pressure group: the power is in the Spirit, and when we withdraw our faith, hope, confidence, or fear and place our entire reliance on the Invisible, "the checks exist, and will appear" for "the dice of God are always loaded."

But these checks do not appear as long as man places his hope, confidence, and reliance on man, or as long as he fears man. They only begin to operate in the lives of those who have come to the realization that Jesus had when he stood before Pilate: "Thou couldest have no power at all against me, except it were given thee from above,"[3] for there is no power in the visible form: The power is in the invisible Essence, the substance and law of all form.

For ninety years, now, metaphysical healings have taken place by the very recognition of the truth that power is not in form or effect, that germs do not carry power, that weather and climate do not have power, but that all power is in the Invisible. Those who have been living in that consciousness have avoided, not necessarily all the evils or ills of this world, but perhaps eighty per cent of them, and that is a satisfactory beginning in this very first century of the understanding and application of spiritual laws.

Since everything that takes place in your life or mine has to take place first within our consciousness, it is within our own consciousness that we have to come into an agreement that the law of *as ye sow so shall ye reap* is operating, a law that eventually does put down the overbearing. There is a law—you cannot name it, you cannot see it, hear it, taste it, touch it, or smell it, but it exists—and it has in the end brought down every evil or tyrannical form of government that has ever been set up. It has torn down every person who has gotten out of hand, who has become too big for his breeches, whose head has grown too big for his own hat. Every such person has been brought down to earth, and as you have already seen, during this past generation, it does not take forever!

Somewhere in this world a beginning will have to be made to bring about God's government on earth. You have all witnessed that God's government on earth has not been brought about by praying for it, for of praying there has been no end. Moreover, it can never be brought about on earth by a continuation of the strife that has long existed among churches. God's government will only be brought about in the same way that you can bring about health, supply, and companionship in your own life; and that is not by going out and believing that you are going to get God to do something for you or that some new religion, some new teaching, or holding to some thought is going to bring God into your life; but in the realization that the only real law is a spiritual law and that material and mental laws are not law and operate as law only while there is a belief in them, a conviction of them, or a hope or faith in them.

In proportion then as you come to see that the things, the conditions, and the persons whom you have feared have had power in your experience only as long as you have permitted them to be power, and that you could bring an end to that at any time that you recognized the Invisible, you will bear witness and be a beholder. If you can look out on this world scene and realize that you have no reason to fear "man, whose breath is in his nostrils,"[4] you will have no reason to fear even a thousand united men.

On this point of *unitedness,* do not forget that there have been combinations of men, combinations of states, combinations of countries, and none of them has survived. Every combination has ultimately fallen because strength is not in union: strength is only in oneness; strength is only in the realization of one Being, one Power, one Law.

That is why in this work one individual can become a light. He becomes a light unto his family, unto his community, and if he wishes to dedicate himself to the spiritual life, he can be a light to an entire universe, because it takes only the dedication to a principle—not the dedication to man, but the dedication to a principle—to live inwardly in the continuous realization:

I need not fear "man, whose breath is in his nostrils," and certainly I must have no faith in man, for I am convinced of an invisible Life, an invisible Law, and an invisible Being.

The Conviction of God Removes Fear

All that it takes for us to attain freedom from fear is a conviction that there is a God. Whether you believe it or not, there are not many persons who believe that there is a God. When asked, they usually say, "I believe in God," but they really don't. Few persons do. Wherever there is a conviction that there is a God, there is no fear, because the very word itself must signify Omnipotence, Infinity, Eternality, and that would leave nothing to fear. It signifies Omnipresence, and that would instantly remove fear of anything whether appearing as a person, a political party, a group of any kind, or anything else—even an ideology. Who could fear an ideology in the presence of God? Who could fear bombs in the presence of God?

Nothing can ever be power in the presence of God. If this were not true, there would be no God, or God would be on a finite, human, or limited level. This would not be God because the word itself must give to us a feeling of omnipotence, omnipresence, and omniscience, and in that realization, all fear goes, and when the fear has gone, the object of the fear disappears.

Always when fear goes, the object of fear goes, because the object of fear is only fear itself externalized, and there cannot be fear in the presence of a realization of spiritual law. Spiritual law does not overcome other laws. Spiritual law, being infinite and omnipotent, is the only law. What has probably made this difficult to understand throughout these years is that spiritual law is not evident to human sight, to hearing, taste, touch, or smell, and can be observed only by its effects. It becomes important, therefore, to look back and see how inevitable is the downfall and destruction of whatever is wrong.

"There is always some leveling circumstance that puts down the overbearing." Emerson does not define or explain it. He simply states, "There is always a leveling circumstance"–and there is! The leveling circumstance is God, spiritual law, and he rightly concludes that "the dice of God are always loaded."

Effects of the Evolutionary Process at Work in Consciousness

If you have sufficient discernment to see how the world has improved in the last fifty, sixty, or seventy years and how much permanent good has come into this world in the area of man's relationship with man, and in nations' relationships with nations, you would realize how close we are to the end of all national and international disputes–not to the differences existing among nations, because that can never be.

As long as we are human beings, in certain minor areas of human activity, there will always be differences of opinion and differences of interest, but look about you and observe the changes that have come into this world already in commercial and international relationships, and you will see that in the over-all picture there has been a gradual elimination of many of the evils that existed years ago and there has also been a gradual coming into focus of more harmonious relationships on a permanent basis. We are now probably witnessing an end to these overbearing peoples or nations as the adjustment is being made to eliminate some of the evils that have existed for the past two or three hundred years.

Undoubtedly, evolution is doing its work. Undoubtedly, this silent Infinite Invisible is operating in human consciousness, bringing about changes. We are now really going through a period of adjustment as gradually many evils are disappearing. But we can hasten the day, not only for ourselves individually—which is not of too great importance except that what occurs in our consciousness affects the demonstration of the entire world—but for the world by the overcoming of our fear through the realization of the Infinite Invisible, which is a Presence and a Power that is overturning and overturning and overturning "until he come whose right it is."[5] There is an Invisible.

You would be surprised what a great contribution you could make to the world by not going out into the world to fight these so-called evils, but by having additional periods of meditation for the realization of the impotency and impersonal nature of these evils. Instead of fighting men, fighting churches or political parties, sit home and realize the powerless nature of these. Let others do the fighting, and let them discover, as people did in ancient days, that the enemy fights and destroys itself. It does, if only we do not enter the battle, but sit on the sidelines in the realization of the impotence of those who appear to be the overbearing.

Since this work began, the major premise has always been the realization that there is an Invisible—an Infinite Invisible—and through that realization I personally have been able to withdraw from the battles of the world. I have been able to withdraw from the battle of earning a living, of competing, and even the battle which might be involved in carrying this Message out to the world. But there is no battle connected with this Message: no proselyting, no fighting, no arguing. There is only an inner realization that the might of the world is invisible—and not only invisible, but that it is good—and then comes a relaxing from either physical or mental fighting to give It the opportunity to come forth into expression; whereas to engage in might or power, physical might or mental power, is to ignore the greatest Force there is in life: the greatest Power, the All-power, the only Power, and that which is the real Power.

All this has been misunderstood because the same words have different meanings for different persons. When Gandhi spoke of nonresistance, the world thought that he meant doing nothing, but he did not mean anything of the sort, as we well know by the results of that nonresistance. It was not through doing nothing that the freedom of India was brought about. Gandhi was not doing nothing: he was doing something so constructive that it did what all the years of struggling and fighting never had been able to accomplish.

So it is. The United States had a Civil War that was supposed to have freed the Negro. It never really did. Only now are Negroes finding their freedom in this country. They were not freed through a war; they could be freed only through the evolution of consciousness. The freedom they gained from the Civil War was the freedom from being sold on a block; but aside from that, they were kept in somewhat the same state of slavery they had struggled against before the War between the States: work from sunup to sundown with little or no remuneration. The Civil War did not change that condition. Evolution, the operation of the Invisible, led the Negro step by step until now at last he is coming into a greater measure of freedom.

So it has been for years. Wars have never accomplished any good purpose, but there is a silent, invisible Force operating and performing Its function of freedom: freedom, abundance, literacy, and all those things that we know to be necessary and good.

Give Up Fear and Faith and Attain Grace

No one can define that in which he has faith: he can only feel that there is an Invisible. I feel and see It as I look out into the trees in Hawaii, seeing them one day without coconuts, and a few days or weeks later with coconuts, wondering why and how this is possible and then realizing that there is an invisible Power overcoming gravity, overcoming resistance, and bringing forth almost from a nothingness something appearing outwardly as very solid form. You, too, can see it in your gardens as you watch your bushes without flowers one day and then in a short time laden with blossoms, and realize that there is an Invisible operating, bringing forth after Its own image and likeness.

To fear man, circumstances, or conditions is to worship idols. So also to have faith in men is to make idols. But to understand that there is a spiritual Invisible, a divine Law in operation, a Love, a Life, a Presence, a Power, and then to rest back and let It function without the use of physical or mental force: this is the Grace that brings about the changes in our human experience; this is the power of Grace coming into expression.

What is this Grace of which we speak? It cannot be defined. It is not something earned or won; It has to be felt. The power of Grace is the power of the Invisible. It is something we bring into expression by the withdrawal of fear of, and faith in, "man, whose breath is in his nostrils,"[6] and then when there is no longer fear or faith, the power of Grace can come into expression and bring forth everything and everyone needed in our experience.

Except to students who have studied for a long while, it is not possible to explain Grace, because Grace actually is the operation of a law that can function only in the consciousness of those who have put up the sword, and who have also laid aside their faith in man, in documents, in unions, or in unitedness. For some this is too difficult because they must know the how, the why, and the wherefore of everything, and it is hopeless to expect these persons to understand anything as intangible as Grace until they have come to a place of rising above that which can be explained through reason.

I know less about the workings of the Spirit than perhaps anybody else in the world because I know nothing about it. I only know this: It works! However It works, It works when there is no fear and even when there is no faith: when there is not even faith in right thinking, not even faith in holding a right thought, not even faith that God can do something, when there is just no fear and no faith, but only the realization of a divine

Grace. Man has blocked Grace from operating because of his fears and his faith. He fears effect or he has faith in effect, and that is the one thing that blocks the operation of the Invisible in his experience.

You can watch how this functions because if you lose only a little of your faith in human reliances—men, churches, or political parties—if you lose only a little fear of some alien ideology and if you lose only a little faith in the people and things in which you have heretofore had faith and rest in the Invisible, you will see right from the beginning how some measure of change begins to take place in your experience.

None of us has attained full and complete freedom for the simple reason that we cannot attain full and complete release from fear and faith. The reason is that neither this fear nor this faith is personal. It is a universal miasma, a universal hypnotism, and as much as we might individually overcome it, there still will be enough of the universal operating so that, as I said before, even the most dedicated find that they are not one hundred per cent free from the sins and diseases of the world, although many of them attain a measure of freedom. The full and complete freedom can only come as the degree of universal fear and faith is lessened.

You would be surprised if you could experience the simplicity of achieving meditation, once you have neither fear nor faith. You would be surprised how easy it is to settle back into a meditation when you have nothing and nobody to fear, and when you are not looking even to a God with faith, when you can settle back in the complete realization of IS. "The Lord is my shepherd"[7]—I shall not fear. "The Lord is my shepherd." The Infinite Invisible *is,* and It is operating. Because I know this, I find it easier to accept Emerson's statement that "the dice of God are always loaded," and to let God and his loaded dice take the responsibility for governing the world.

We owe a great debt to Emerson—greater than we know, and this is one debt for which I will give him a little extra handshake when I meet him: "The dice of God are always loaded." Isn't it comforting to realize that the overbearing are brought down, individually and collectively?

The minute you can go into meditation realizing that you are not going there to get anything, nor to get any power, that there is nothing you need, for whatever is in the Invisible already is, instantly you are free from human thought, and you can settle down into a tabernacling and an inner communion. Watch and see if it is not true that the only thing that interferes with your attainment of meditation is that either good or evil will come into your mind, either the desire to get rid of evil or to get good, and that can only be overcome through the realization of this Invisible.

You could throw every worry aside and never again know a sleepless night . . . in the conviction that there is nothing good or evil *in and of itself.* . . .

What creates and perpetuates humanhood is the pairs of opposites—the belief that flowers are good but that weeds are evil, the belief that robins are good but the bugs on the rosebushes are evil. If, however, we neither gloss over some evil appearance as good, which is merely an old metaphysical cliché, nor judge it bad, but recognize that all that exists is pure Soul, infinitely expressing Itself, eventually even the bugs on the rosebushes find their rightful place where they cannot perform any destructive function. Even the so-called evil people of the world begin to serve a good purpose—they do, or they are removed from positions where they can work their purposes.

We are approaching a period in the world in which evil will find no room for expression in people, thoughts, and things. It will be crowded right off the earth, because the earth will be so full of the knowledge of this principle of one power that evil will have no channel through which to function. It will be lopped off as fast as it shows its head by this invisible spiritual power that permeates consciousness.[8]

Nothing shall by any manner or means harm you, and not a thing in the world is going to do good for you. Being still will not do it, being noisy will not prevent it: it is a matter of realization. Is there an Invisible, and is the karmic law inevitable? As ye sow, so shall ye reap! Then, let the evil doers do their sowing: they will do their reaping, and some day awaken.

Across the Desk

That the Infinite Way is reaching human consciousness through many streams you already know. It remains only for me to remind you that the healing consciousness is developed through the understanding and practice of specific principles which have been revealed to us and which are proving themselves over and over again.

For serious study, please take the chapter "Breaking the Fetters That Bind You," from *The Infinite Way Letters of 1958*[9] and work diligently with this material every day for at least a month, and then watch as new experiences unfold.

~8~

CONTEMPLATION DEVELOPS THE BEHOLDER

Many times the young student is likely to believe that the spiritual or contemplative way of life is a life without discipline, but the very opposite of this is true, because there is no life that requires greater discipline than does the spiritual life.

Life, as it is lived by most persons, is more or less undisciplined because little or no attempt is made by the individual to control the nature of his thinking. He is prone to accept everything that he sees or hears, usually rejoicing over what he thinks is good and moaning over what he believes to be evil, so that seldom does anyone ask himself, "Is this as good as it appears to be?" or, "Is this as evil as it appears to be?" Rather are appearances accepted in accordance with human judgment. In the spiritual way of life, however, that cannot be done because the entire spiritual life is based on the rejection of appearances.

Judge Not After Appearances

Commonly accepted metaphysics today teaches the rejection and denial of the appearance of evil and the realization of its unreal nature. But in the truly spiritual life, we have to go beyond merely rejecting evil as error because we also have to deny reality to that which appears as good; we have to unsee the humanly good appearances to the same degree that we unsee the humanly evil ones. Spiritually discerned, there is neither good nor evil, and it is on this premise that the entire spiritual universe is built. The discipline on this path lies in rejecting every appearance, whether it is good or evil, in the realization that whatever it is that is of God is invisible to the human senses.

"Why callest thou me good? there is none good but one, that is, God.[1] . . . Neither do I condemn thee."[2] In other words, there is no sitting in judgment on what appears to be evil, but neither is there any acceptance of the appearance of good: there is a recognition that the only real is the Invisible—the spiritual—and that is something that cannot be seen with the eyes, nor heard with the ears.

Under the old metaphysics, if we were confronted with an appearance and judged it to be evil, we immediately had to resist it: overcome, destroy, or remove it. If, on the other hand, we were confronted with an appearance of human good, we accepted it and rejoiced over it. The danger in this procedure, however, is that the very thing that appears to be good may, in and of itself, be evil, or may change to evil, or its effect upon one may be of an evil nature.

A very good illustration of this is that nearly everybody would agree that having a million dollars—earning or inheriting it—is good, and yet the acquisition of a million dollars has proved to be the ruination of many persons. It has changed their nature and made them grasping because, when some persons who have had little or nothing and who have always been free and joyous in sharing that little acquire more than they have been accustomed to having, many of them begin to hoard and grasp it and lay it up for a rainy day, fearing to spend it, so that what would appear to have been good has turned out to be evil for them.

In the human picture practically everyone, almost without exception, rejoices at a birth and sorrows at a death. Nevertheless, more trouble has been caused in the world by birth than ever has been caused by death. So, if we were to judge from human appearances, we would be struck by the tragedies that take place as a result of birth, despite all the rejoicing, and by the uselessness and futility of much of the sorrowing at death.

These are extreme illustrations of how unwise it is to judge of good or evil. Spiritually, however, judging as to good or evil goes far beyond being unwise. In a spiritual sense, it is absolutely wrong because there is a Power that is within each and every one of us, and this Power has as Its function the creating, maintaining, and sustaining of harmony in our existence, and when for any reason harmony is apparently taken from our lives, Its function is to restore it.

Living as a Witness to the Activity of God

This Power or Principle is illustrated fully in the experience of Jesus Christ as narrated in the four Gospels. Jesus clearly revealed that his function was to heal the sick, raise the dead, feed the hungry, and forgive the sinner. Always he said, "I can of mine own self do nothing.[3] . . . the Father that dwelleth in me, he doeth the works."[4] He always bore witness to the presence of

God. In every one of the miracles performed by the Master, there was the denial of self and the glorification of the Father. Always it was, "I of my own self am doing nothing, for I of my own self am nothing. If I speak of myself, I bear witness to a lie. Therefore, it is not I who am good, it is not I who do the healing: I am but bearing witness to the presence and power of God."

How can we bear witness to this Power except by being still? If we do otherwise, we can no longer say that we are doing nothing or that we are nothing. We have become something the moment we do something. Therefore, when we are confronted with appearances—whether the appearance is called good or evil—we are being confronted with a human appearance, and if we would bear witness to the presence of God, we must do nothing, we must think nothing, and we must have no judgment. I am sure that you will not confuse this with an ignoring of our life's work, nor as a lazy do-nothing attitude, but you will understand this to be a disciplined withholding of judging as to good or evil and an attitude of expectancy—as of listening within. Be sure that you understand the significance of this attitude.

In order to make ourselves nothing, we must immediately realize within ourselves, "There is neither good nor evil: there is only God." Then, as we look out at the erroneous appearance with no judgment, there truly is neither good nor evil: there is only the presence of God, and now the Father within can perform Its function, and Its function is to dissolve the appearance and reveal God's glory—reveal Its own being.

Even though to our sense a healing appears, it is not really a healing: it is the dissolving of the material picture, and the bringing to visibility of the spiritual one.

There is only one way in which that can be done, and that is to withhold judgment as to good or evil, and then let the Father within do the work. Then, and then only, can we truthfully feel that we have had nothing to do with the demonstration except to bear witness to God in action.

This reminds me of a woman who was healed of a disease that had been pronounced incurable, and her husband, out of deep gratitude, went to the practitioner and offered him a check as a token of appreciation. When he began to express his gratitude, the practitioner said, "Oh, I didn't do it—God did it," at which the man put the check back in his pocket and replied, "Oh, well, then I don't owe you anything. I'll give the check to God."

As a matter of fact, insofar as the healing was concerned, the practitioner was right, but the husband was also right. The practitioner had not brought about the healing: he had merely borne witness to God in action, so therefore there was no money due because of the healing. Where the husband was wrong was that he should have known that if the practitioner had not been available and had not been able to bear witness to God's grace, there would have been no healing. If the practitioner had been dependent for his livelihood on hanging telephone wires, tending furnaces, or whatever else his job might have been, he perhaps might not have been able to live in the Spirit and to bear witness to God when called upon. Giving him money, therefore, was not for the healing. It was merely to enable him to be free of other obligations so that he could keep his consciousness clear and free of entanglements and could always be in the Spirit to bear witness to Its activity.

When you witness healing works, always remember what it is you are witnessing. You are not witnessing the power of an individual, for an individual has no such power: you are merely witnessing an individual who is keeping himself free of the appearance-world and maintaining himself in a consciousness of no judgment, so that the grace of God can come through, because the grace of God cannot come through the human mind. And what is the human mind but anybody's mind that is still indoctrinated with the belief in two powers?

Discipline in the Contemplative Life

Regardless of how much knowledge of truth a person may have, no matter how many years he may have studied truth, he may still have no healing power. It is not how many statements of truth a person knows intellectually, or can declare. Healing power has to do with the degree of the actual awareness and conviction attained of the nonpower of appearances. It is for this reason that the spiritual path is a path of discipline, and every disciple or student must begin at some moment in his career to withhold judgment.

In proportion as this consciousness of no judgment is attained, the appearances in this world automatically change as they touch your consciousness. This is because your consciousness is not reacting to good or to evil, and is, therefore, able to pierce the veil of illusion, even the veil of good illusion, and see that there is nothing to fear and nothing to gloat about because what you are seeing is not the spiritual creation, but a finite concept of it, sometimes good and sometimes bad, sometimes rich and sometimes poor, sometimes healthy and sometimes sick, sometimes alive and sometimes dead. But none of that is true of God's kingdom.

The Master's statement, "My kingdom is not of this world,"[5] helps us to discipline ourselves. Instantly we shut out everything that we see or hear, realizing that that is *this world,* but it is not *My* kingdom, the Christ-kingdom, the spiritual kingdom; and therefore, we neither love, hate, nor fear it. Think of the discipline involved in refraining from all attempts to change the appearance when we are in the midst of what seems to be a problem for ourselves or another. Think, think of any discordant appearance that you have ever seen, heard, tasted, touched, or smelled; see the discipline that is necessary to refrain from attempting to alter, change, or do something about it; and then be convinced and know, "My kingdom—the place where I live, move, and have my being—is not of this world. Therefore, I have nothing to do about this world except to know that it is not of *My* kingdom."

As we withdraw judgment—which means to withdraw our hate, fear, or love of the appearance—it is then that this Invisible, the Spirit of God, which is in us, can immediately go to work to change the appearance.

Self-Preservation Is the Dominant Note in Human Experience

When the disciples were afraid because of the storm at sea, they awakened the Master, but he did not attempt to stop the storm by praying to God because he knew that he was being faced with an illusory appearance. He merely "rebuked the wind, and said unto the sea, Peace, be still. And the wind ceased, and there was a great calm." [6] What the disciples were seeing was something more than a storm: they were probably not aware of it, but they were seeing a selfhood apart from God, and above all they may have been afraid that they were going to lose their lives.

The disciples, seized as they were by fear, were responding as most people do to that first law of nature, the law of self-preservation. In the human picture, that law (if we can dignify it by the name of law) is responsible for most of the evil that is in the world. A person would not steal if it were not that he is trying to preserve his personal and human sense of life. He is hoping to keep himself from starving or from being a failure, and he is staving off lack and limitation. In short, he is preserving his own human sense of identity.

What but self-preservation lies behind every war? Men call it patriotism because they claim that wars are fought to preserve the nation, but a nation is only a group of individuals, so in the final analysis it is the preservation and perpetuation of themselves, of their human lives and human supply, that induces them to enter into a war. The horror of it is, however, that people are always willing to sacrifice and send their children off to get killed, as long as they can stay home and be saved. Children are not as important to most people as they themselves are. The children must go off and get killed or wounded or demented so that others can stay home and have abundance.

In the storm, then, the disciples were not really afraid of the storm. What difference would a storm have made to them, if they had not believed that their lives were in danger? Who cares whether the wind is forty or a hundred miles an hour, if there is no danger to one's life or limb? It is only while there is fear of the loss of life that anybody cares whether the storm rages or ceases.

Many of us would be able to attain our release from the world of cause and effect, that is, from the world of appearances, if only we could bring to bear upon the situation that great assurance of the Master, "It is I; be not afraid." To know this truth would immediately divest us of any judgment as to the nature of the appearance.

"It is I; be not afraid"–I, *God, is the only life;* I, *God, is the life of individual being, and that Life cannot be lost and It cannot be destroyed. Let the storm do what it will. I cannot fear.*

Similarly, who cares how many germs there are in the world, unless we can be made to believe that germs can destroy our life? Ah! That sets up an antagonism in us, and we are going out now to wipe all the germs off the face of the earth. Why? What have we against germs? Nothing! Except that they threaten destruction to our own lives, or our own health!

But suppose we came to the realization that our life is indestructible, that neither life nor death can separate us from God? Now what difference would germs make? And in that realization, the battle against error–that particular form of error–would cease, and none of these things would move us:

"None of these things move me."[7] *My life is God; my life is in God; my life is with God; and neither life nor death can separate me from God.*

In that realization, death itself has no longer any fears or terrors. No one can possibly fear death once he realizes that neither death nor life can separate him from the Life that he is, the Life that is his being.

The Detachment of a Beholder

If we accept the Master's statement, "My kingdom is not of this world,"[8] we do not have to fight, remove, or overcome anything in the external world:

"It is I; be not afraid."[9] I *am the life of you;* I, *God, the Spirit of God in you is your life, your being, and the substance of your body.*

When we are no longer afraid of anything in the external world, then we automatically arrive at a state of consciousness that no longer concerns itself with the good appearances or fears the evil appearances, but looks out at them with a sense of detachment as an onlooker or a beholder, with no interest in changing, improving, or destroying them: with just the attitude of a beholder.

In this attitude of a beholder, our personal mental powers come to a stop, and it is as if we were watching a sunrise or a sunset. Nobody in his right mind believes that he can hasten the rising of the sun or its setting, or that he can increase its beauty. Therefore, in watching a sunrise or a sunset, we become completely the beholder, watching nature at work, watching God at work. We never enter into the picture, never seek to change, remove, destroy, or attempt to improve it in any way. As a beholder, we are always in the absolute center of our own being; and as a beholder, we can truthfully say, "What a beautiful sunset," or, "What a beautiful sunrise God is bringing about."

If we were in an art gallery, standing before the works of the great masters, we would be beholders because all that we would be trying to do would be to draw from the picture what the artist had placed there. We do not try to improve the picture; we do not try to destroy it: all that we seek to do is to draw forth from the picture what the artist has created and placed there for our enjoyment. We do not enter the picture: we behold it. If we enter anything, it would be the consciousness of the artist to behold exactly what he beheld because we are now of one consciousness—one mind.

When we hear a symphony, we do not enter the symphony: We stand off as a beholder, this time listening, listening to what the composer had in mind. We are not trying to improve his work, nor are we trying to destroy it: we are merely trying to understand it. Even if it sounds like bad music to us—unpleasant, discordant, or offbeat—we still do not try to change it: We stand still, without judgment, trying to grasp what the composer had in mind, and it would not be surprising if eventually we found ourselves right inside the consciousness of that composer, hearing the music as he heard it when he put it on paper. Then we would have the same understanding of it that he had.

So it is that God created this universe and all that is therein, and it is good! To our finite sense, however, we see some of this universe as evil and some of it as good, and strangely enough, the man right beside us may be seeing what we call good as evil; what we see as evil he may be seeing as good; so therefore, we cannot be seeing this universe the way God made it. We are seeing it through our ignorance of God, our lack of God-awareness, just as we might see a painting or hear music and because of our ignorance be unable to discern what the artist or the composer had in mind.

As we look out at this world of appearances *without judgment,* it is as if we were realizing that God's Spirit made all that is, and made it spiritual, and in that realization we now behold a spiritual universe, even though at the moment we do not understand or see it the way the Grand Architect of the universe created it. We cannot see through the eyes of Him who designed and formed this universe while we are looking out of human eyes, but by looking at this world without judgment, it is as if we were trying to see what God created, as God sees it, in other words, entering into the consciousness of God.

The only way we can do that is to withhold judgment and be still, seeing neither good nor evil, being a beholder, and letting the Father present the picture to us. We just bear witness; we just behold—but not with the idea of healing anyone, not with the idea of improving or enriching anyone—merely with the idea of beholding the picture as God made it and as God sees it.

Withhold Judgment as to Good or Evil

The only way that the mind of God can be consciously expressed through us is when we are withholding human judgment as to good or evil and letting ourselves be beholders, and then the Spirit of God lives in and through us, changing the picture from what it seems to be, and revealing to us that which was always there, even though finite sense could not discern it.

Flowers, beautiful and colorful as they are, actually have no color. We are not seeing the flowers as they are, because color does not exist. There are light waves, and when they strike our eyes, we interpret the rate of

their vibration as color. A certain vibration is inter-
preted as red, another as purple, and another as blue.
It is color only when it touches our eyesight, and if our
eyesight is not accurate, we may see one color as red,
whereas another person may see it as quite a different
color.

It is the same with sound. If, in a forest, the largest
tree were to topple over, there would never be a sound
heard in that forest because no sound is taking place.
There are invisible sound waves set up by the falling
tree, but the silence is absolute and complete until it
touches an eardrum. Those sound waves must touch an
eardrum before there can be any sound, and if they
touched an impaired eardrum, there would still be no
sound, no matter how loud the sound might seem to be
to you.

We are always judging by the limitation of our finite
senses. We are not seeing this world as it is: we are
seeing this world as our mind interprets it. In some parts
of the world, people go about naked, and in that kind of
a civilization nobody thinks there is anything wrong
about it. The fact is that being clothed or unclothed is a
concept of life that has evolved, not life itself. The Father
said, "Who told thee that thou wast naked?"[10]

As we live the life of contemplation, therefore, we
find ourselves gradually withdrawing judgment from
appearances, and when we see, or when we are told
about erroneous appearances, we do not react to them,
and they do not register in our consciousness, and, as far
as they are concerned, our mind is a blank. We have no
desire to change, alter, or improve the appearance
presented to us: we are just beholders waiting for God to
reveal it to us as it is.

"Awake Thou That Sleepest"[11]

"I shall be satisfied, when I awake, with thy likeness."[12] A spiritually awakened person is completely satisfied with the people of this world because he knows them as they really are, and even though he sees the discords and problems that they are experiencing, he also knows that these are no part of their real being, but only a part of that educated sense which is trying to preserve an already immortal life, or trying to get more supply for one who is, and always has been, joint heir with Christ in God. Therefore, he looks with compassion on those whom he knows are in ignorance of their true identity or those who do not understand the nature of God's world.

Suppose you come to the realization that "I and my Father are one,"[13] that the life of God is your individual life and therefore your life is indestructible, and that neither life nor death can ever separate you from God, which is life eternal and immortal. Now you begin to lose your fear of death, you begin to lose your fear of the burglar with a gun in his hand because you know that you have no life to lose. No longer do you fear for your life. Your life is now recognized as God—indestructible, immortal, and eternal. Death? Even death cannot separate you from God.

"Awake thou that sleepest,"[14] and learn that God is your life. Neither life nor death can take your life from you. Life goes on whether you live in the East or the West; it goes on whether you live in this house or that house; it goes on whether you are young or old, or even whether you have gone into the realm beyond. Life is a continuous experience because life is God, and God is life.

The Contemplative Life Brings a Consciousness of Life as Indestructible

Through the contemplative life, you come to a whole new state of consciousness in which, while you are still aware that there are evils in the world, no longer do you sit in judgment on them or condemn them, no longer do you misunderstand them. Now you have compassion because you understand why they are taking place. Furthermore, you know that they must continue to take place in each person's experience until he is awakened.

When an individual is awakened to the fact that life is indestructible, immortal, and eternal, he cannot fear death; and once he no longer fears death, he cannot know death. No one can experience anything that is not a part of his consciousness, and when death is no longer a part of consciousness, he cannot die.

Leave this scene? Yes! Yes! That is like a bouquet of flowers. In a few days the form of the flowers will perish, but not their life. The life will go on and be manifested in other forms of the same kind of flowers, and it will be the same life. It will not be a different life. The life that is in a bouquet of roses today or the life that was in roses ten thousand years ago is the same life.

Your life and your identity and your consciousness will still be here ten thousand years from now, but in a different form. You will not be gone: only your form will change. That this is true is evidenced by the fact that when you came into this world, you weighed six, seven, eight, nine, or ten pounds, but that form has been changing ever since. Even the form of the organs of the body has changed. Organs not developed when we were born have developed and matured, and some of these at a certain age stop functioning, but we go on just the same: there is no change in us. We are the same person, the same life, the same consciousness, despite the changes that take place in our bodies. The child-body is not that of the adult-body, and the body of the aged is not the same as the body of the adult; but the individual is the same, the life is the same, the Soul is the same, the consciousness is the same. Only the outer form changes.

So it will be that, unless I am lifted out of this life, I will be here a thousand years from now, even though the form may be different. As a matter of fact, the sex could be different, and the reason is that *I*–and this applies to every one of us–*I* has no sex. Once you become aware of the *I* that you are, you will find It completely independent of body and completely independent of sex, manifesting as either sex, even though it will still be *I*. That is because *I* is spiritual; *I* is one with God; *I* is of the nature of God. Therefore, *I* is without finite form, yet *I* can manifest as, in, or through finite form. When you have realized that, the sting of death leaves you because you will know then that you are *I*, and *I* will always be your state of consciousness, except that you will progressively elevate until there is nothing finite left.

That *I* is the secret of the transcendental life. With the realization, "It is I; be not afraid,"[15] and that that *I* is God, all fear goes, all judgment, all condemnation, and then even as you look out upon the world and witness the discords that hold mankind in bondage, the feeling is there: "Just think, if the people of this world could awaken to their true identity!" and that is all there is to it. They are not evil; they are not bad: They are just fulfilling the law of self-preservation, and so we do not sit in judgment on them because we have done the same thing.

"It Is I; Be Not Afraid"

When we throw a bomb at somebody else—an atomic bomb or a bomb of hatred or gossip—or if we kill in self-defense, we are doing just what the world is doing: we are operating from the standpoint of the law of self-preservation, and the self we are trying to preserve is a finite sense of self that has no contact with God. That is why we are trying to save it. If we understood our true identity as one with God, we would not have to try to save it. God can govern and care for His own universe.

In the face of danger, we withdraw judgment and realize, "Whatever is real is God-maintained and God-sustained. Whatever is real is of God, and it is permanent and eternal. I do not have to lift my finger to save it, to preserve it, or to do anything about it. I merely have to behold God in action." We must sit, not in judgment but completely without judgment, in the realization that this is God's universe.

"It is I; be not afraid.[16] . . . *My kingdom is not of this world"* [17] *—My kingdom is intact. All that God has joined together, no man can put asunder. My Father's life and my life are one; therefore my life cannot be put asunder by sin, by disease, by lack, by death, by war, or by any other means. Nothing can put asunder my life, because my life is joined to God's life: it is one with God: God maintains my life eternally, immortally, and neither life nor death can separate life from itself or change that relationship.*

In the face of danger of any nature, we stand by without judgment and bear witness to God. Then afterward, when the harmony has been restored and safety and security realized, we can repeat with the Master, "I of my own self did nothing. The Father within me did the work." Now, of course, there was one thing we did that was very important and very difficult, and that was to come to the place of being a beholder. The discipline of the spiritual path consists of the ability to discipline one's self so as not to see a picture that has to be changed, altered, improved, or removed, and the vision to look out at the pictures this world presents with this conviction, "It is I; be not afraid," and then stand still and bear witness while God brings about the transformation of the visible scene.

"It is I; be not afraid.[18] . . . My kingdom is not of this world.[19] . . . Cease ye from man, whose breath is in his nostrils: for wherein is he to be accounted of?"[20] These are the three scriptural passages that have been the foundation of my healing work ever since the early 1930's. Before that, I was doing healing work, but without knowing why or how, or what the principle was. It was, you might say, just a gift of God. But in the early 1930's, I was given the revelation of those three statements.

"Cease ye from man, whose breath is in his nostrils: for wherein is he to be accounted of?" Do not try to change man, improve him, or heal him, and certainly do not judge or condemn him: take no account of him. In other words, be still!

Then came, "My kingdom is not of this world." Therefore, do not judge by the appearance of this world, because in *My* kingdom, harmony is. *My* kingdom is a spiritual kingdom, and heaven is established even on earth as it is in heaven. Again you cease from all attempts to change, improve, heal, or reform.

The secret of the success that I have had in my work in prisons is in going to the prison without any desire to reform any body, not blinding myself to the fact that humanly these men and women were not living up to a spiritual standard, but realizing that whatever they had done had been done because of the urgency of the law of self-preservation, because of ignorance of their true identity. Therefore, there was no more condemnation for them than a schoolteacher has for a student who comes to learn. He knows in advance that his student does not know what he is going to learn from the teacher, but he does not condemn the student for that. He recognizes that the student is ignorant and he is going to change that ignorance by imparting knowledge.

So it is that when I have gone into prisons, I have not condemned or judged: I have realized, "Here are people in ignorance of the fact that God is their life, and that they do not have to sustain it. God is their supply, and they do not have to get supply. They are joint heirs with Christ in God." So my work has been to enlighten them as to their true identity because once they know that, their whole nature will be changed.

As human beings, there is not one of us without sin, whether in the act of commission or in the act of desiring. We are transformed in only one way: by coming into the awareness of our true identity, and then learning to be still and knowing that "I am God," and that because *I* is God, that *I* governs Its own universe; It maintains it and It sustains it. In fact, that *I* is the bread and the meat, and the wine, and the water unto Its creation; and therefore, each one of us has *I*, each one of us has in the midst of him, closer than breathing, that which the Master says is the mission of the Father within, that which heals, saves, redeems, resurrects, and feeds. That *I,* each one of us has, and It is the Christ. In the awareness of that *I,* we become beholders of the Christ in action, and as beholders of the Christ in action, we are able to pierce the veil of illusion, and then instead of seeing the ugly picture that the human mind has drawn, we begin to see reality.

Across the Desk

Today, world news holds the spotlight wherever one travels, and wherever there is world news, there is fear and anxiety. The past centuries in which this world has lived without spiritual intercession have made men lose their hope that God can save, but the century that has brought forth great spiritual healing ministries will also reveal the nature and activity of spiritual power in the wider affairs of mankind.

In the minds of most persons concerned with the major problems of the world today, as always, the great desire is for victory. Capitalism seeks a victory over communism and *vice versa;* trade unions want more and greater victories over the very source of their incomes, while on the other hand there are still some unenlightened capitalists with dreams of victories over labor.

Neither the Republican Party nor the Democratic Party, Labour or Conservative, Socialist or Liberal wants the peace and prosperity of nations but rather victory over each other.

Who but the blind can believe that the United States, England, and France, and their allies won the First and Second World Wars? Look over the list of all of them, and ask, "What price victory?" And yet the life-blood and wealth of all nations continue to be spent in seeking still another victory. But to turn now to spiritual power for victory would be to revert to the pagan teachings of the pre-Christian era.

Does your vision open to a greater scene than victorious armies marching into civilians' homes and hospitals? Can you envision something better than medals for mass slaughter? Will your vision carry you to greater heights than the alternatives of one kind of material force as against another?

Withdraw your gaze from the picture that materialism would paint for you; turn within and see what promise you find as your gaze travels from the scene without to the Kingdom within. What vision do you see when the word *victory* is dropped from thought?

When victory is no longer your goal, spiritual power will reveal itself to you.

~9~

DAILY PREPARATION
FOR SPIRITUAL LIVING

The young student—the beginning student—should realize that there are specific principles that constitute the message of the Infinite Way. If these principles are not understood and practiced, the Infinite Way remains in the category of a philosophy, just an interesting approach to life, something to read about and then put on the shelf. But that is in no sense what the Infinite Way is. The Infinite Way is a living experience, practical for use in everyday life.

It has been said many times, and claimed by many persons, that the teaching of Jesus Christ is so impractical that it could not possibly be adapted to our modern way of life. This seems strange when we remember that, according to biblical accounts, this so-called impractical way of life healed the sick, raised the dead, provided supply for those who needed it, stilled the storm, and brought peace where there had been discord. This way of life has been called impractical, and yet nothing in the religious history of the world has ever been quite so practical as was Jesus' teaching. It was difficult, but it was practical. And so in these modern days, we, too, will find that living as the Master taught is difficult, but also that it is practical.

The fact that a religious teaching can bring about the healing of physical and mental ills, that it can lead to an increased sense of supply and can provide safety and security, that it can bring an inner peace and a release from the world's major problems, and even some solution to these problems, warrants calling that teaching practical.

Students Must Never Advance Beyond the Principles

Although the Infinite Way is one of the most practical of teachings, it is difficult for the beginner because there must be an understanding of the basic principles, and then there must be a practice of them until the student develops an actual consciousness which makes it possible to let go of any strenuous attempts to *make* these principles effective and demonstrable.

The Infinite Way is difficult for advanced students also, but for a different reason. They often forget that the only reason they can be considered advanced students is that they know and practice the basic principles making up the message of the Infinite Way. There is a temptation on the part of some of them, however, to be so far advanced that they attempt to advance beyond the principles, and that is when they experience trouble. In the practice and living of the Infinite Way, I have found that it is impossible to advance beyond the stage of the beginner; it is impossible to advance beyond the understanding and practice of the original, basic principles, and those who feel that they can outgrow these, or that they have gone beyond them, merely succeed in advancing themselves out of the Infinite Way and its practice.

The Infinite Way consists of two basic principles that set it apart from other teachings. First of all, an actual consciousness of the presence of God must be attained because otherwise the teaching remains only in the realm of mental discussion, theory, belief, or knowledge. As long as a student is merely in intellectual agreement with or has a liking for the principles, he has made no substantial progress on the way. He is nowhere at all until he has actually attained some measure of realization of the Presence.

Let me explain it this way: There is an invisible, transcendental Presence, and that means that right where you are, closer to you than breathing, there is this spiritual, invisible, transcendental Presence, there is an actual Spirit, called the Spirit of God, or the Christ, which is only another term for the individualization of the Spirit of God in man.

When Is a Spiritual Experience a Real Experience?

There is this Presence, and it is within you, and you do not have to go to mountains or temples to find it. You can find it sitting in your own home, in a public library, or in any church where there is quiet and peace. Wherever you are, it is literally true that "the place whereon thou standest is holy ground,"[1] and therefore, wherever you are, you can attain the actual experience of this Presence that is within you. Not only you can, but as an Infinite Way student, *you must.* You must attain the awareness, the actual feeling, the actual realization of a divine Presence within you. You will not be able to analyze or dissect It; you will not be able to explain It to your friends or relatives. It is folly even to try to explain It to yourself: it is enough that you can experience It, and then, because of the fruitage of that experience, you will recognize its validity.

There are many, of course, who read about spiritual experiences in the religious literature of the world who delude themselves into believing that they are experiencing the Presence, whereas they are having nothing more nor less than an emotional jag. The religious literature of the world is replete with accounts of persons who are victims of self-hypnosis, who write the most graphic accounts of experiences that are but figments of their imagination, and we who read cannot but question the veracity of some of these stories, feeling within that this has not been a truly spiritual experience. Why do we have such a reaction? Why do we feel this way? Because we observe that there is no practical fruitage resulting from it: there is no peace attained, no harmony or health. None of the experiences of healing and regeneration that have come to the world through the revelation of Jesus Christ come to those who attempt to live permanently on "cloud nine," but fail to keep their feet on the ground.

Those who do attain the experience of the Christ find that it immediately results in setting them free—free from concern. Problems may linger for quite a while, or they may come and then go, and this is the normal, natural experience in life until, through the continued realization of spiritual identity, spiritual life, and spiritual law, one comes to the place described by the Master as the overcoming of the world. But let us not believe that he uttered those words during the first month of his ministry, because even after he was functioning as a rabbi and actively engaged in the spiritual ministry, even after he was performing some of the miracles described in Scripture, Jesus still had to face the three temptations in the wilderness; and they were serious temptations, as serious as any we will ever experience.

Evolving States of Consciousness

All life is a process of evolution. If we study history, we find that we have been slowly evolving from the state of consciousness of the cave man, from the "eye for an eye and a tooth for a tooth" age, from the horrors of nineteenth- and early twentieth-century capitalism to the broader outlook of the present day. Religion has also evolved from the hell-and-damnation days to the more enlightened approach of today. All history is the account of the evolving of consciousness down through the centuries, a consciousness that is still evolving.

So it is that when the Christ, or Spirit of God, is first consciously realized and begins to operate in our experience, it acts in a somewhat similar evolutionary way. It may begin, first of all, merely to detach us from our fears and doubts, or from concern about our problems, so that gradually the problems of life are solved quietly and peacefully, without worry and without fear of being driven to the extremes of nervous exhaustion.

But soon this activity of the Christ begins to act as a leaven in our entire human experience. Our relationships with others begin to be more harmonious, more natural, and more joyous; our efforts, whether in business, art, or a profession, become less arduous and less tiresome—actually more joyous as they also become more fruitful. Conditions of health begin to change, but we do not really realize that there has been any change until one day something may cause us to look back, and suddenly we are aware that for the last three, four, or five years we have not used any medication or even been in need of any, or we may discover that some physical imperfection is no longer present. All this is a gradual process, an evolutionary process, but it leads always to higher and higher states of spiritual awareness, divine consciousness, resulting in peace and harmony on earth.

The attainment of one experience of the Christ is not sufficient to complete the demonstration of our particular life experience. It is true, as we all know, that there have been many in the history of the world who have attained some measure of this realization of the divine Presence, and yet have continued to suffer discords, diseases, injustices, and inequalities; and I am sure that they, themselves, must have wondered why, since this Presence was with them, those outer conditions continued. They must have wondered why, when they had such a sense of inner peace and joy, the outer experiences did not match the inner harmony they felt they had attained. This brings us to the major principle of the Infinite Way.

The Impersonal Source of All Discord

In the days of early metaphysics, it was discovered that the discords of this world are not as real as they appear to be and that they do not have the substance or law that they appear to have. This led later to the discovery that we are dealing, not with personal sin, personal disease, or personal discord, but with a universal source of individual problems. And here is the second basic principle that sets the Infinite Way apart from other teachings: It is not the wrong thinking of an individual, his sins, or his mistakes that cause most of his problems, but a universal something that has been termed by such many and varied names as mortal mind, carnal mind, hypnotism, or mesmerism.

By whatever name it is called, the realization must come that all error—evil, sin, disease, death, lack, limitation, or old age—is but the product of a universal carnal mind, or mortal mind, which can actually be better summed up as the belief in two powers. This belief in two powers, in the power of good and the power of evil, is the source and actually the substance of what is called the mortal or carnal mind. There is no such thing, really, as a mortal mind or a carnal mind; there is no such entity, any more than there is an entity called darkness. There is, however, a universal belief in two powers, and it is this universal belief in two powers that constitutes the carnal mind and is the source of every discord, every disease, every sin, every form of unemployment, and every lack, of whatever name or nature.

Never believe for a moment that the solution to all these problems can be found in the outer world. The forms of these problems will change, but the basic problem remains. For example, we have progressed from the horse-and-buggy days to the automobile day, and are now making rapid strides forward in the air age; but just as there was unemployment in the horse-and-buggy days, so was there unemployment in the automobile age, and now in the airplane age. The point is that the problem of unemployment is not met by means of economic theory or the speculations of sociology, or by any means known to the human mind. The problem of unemployment will be met only when it is understood to be an activity of a belief in two powers, that is, the activity of the carnal mind. Contrariwise, employment will be universal when it is understood to be the activity of God: God fulfilling Itself as individual being.

Capital and labor problems are being solved to some extent by the changing economic system, but the last and final overcoming of these problems will only be through the realization that the problems never existed separate and apart from a belief in two powers. Trace any form of sin that you like, and you will find that it has its source in a belief in either good or evil. Some conditions we think of as evil and some as good, and so the belief of good and evil continues to operate, and as long as it operates in consciousness, it will operate either as good or as evil, as purity or as sin. All disease, too, no matter what form it takes, has its foundation in the belief in two powers. If there were not a belief in an evil power, disease would not be evil, it would not be deadly, and therefore it would not exist.

Is there any way of proving this? The answer is that no form of sin or disease or any unhappy situation could ever be resolved metaphysically or spiritually if there were a law perpetuating these erroneous conditions. If there were laws of discord, inharmony, or disease, these laws could not be overcome merely through the realization that their foundation rested upon a universal belief in two powers.

In the practice of the Infinite Way, whatever measure of success we may have in bringing harmony into the lives of our students is brought about, not by treating each problem differently, as if rheumatism were different from consumption, or a headache different from a muscle ache, or unemployment different from disease, or false appetite different from lack; but by treating any and all of these as impersonal products of the universal belief in two powers, the mesmeric belief in two powers. So, every single claim of human discord, in whatever category, is treated always from this one basis.

Daily Practice Is Essential

Do not be fooled by the form your outer activity may take: we are all students, regardless of whether we are functioning as practitioners, teachers, or lecturers. We are all students, merely functioning at different levels, and if we ever reach the place where we believe that we have advanced beyond the stage of students, we have advanced too far for our own good. I say to you, with all my years of practice behind me, that I would not be prepared when calls come for help if I should fail on any single day of the week to re-establish myself in the consciousness of the Presence and then go further to the realization that whatever problems I meet this day are appearing to me only as mesmeric suggestions based on the universal belief in two powers, and that at the moment they appear I recognize them as the "arm of flesh," and dismiss them as such.

The reason must be clear to you. The Master gave it to us in these words, "I can of mine own self do nothing."[2] Therefore, if I of mine own self can do nothing, there must be Something that does the work; there must be Something functioning in my experience that is responsible for my life and its demonstration. What is it? First of all, it is the realized Presence of the Spirit within; and secondly, it is abiding constantly and consciously in the realization that whatever I am being presented with is a picture—a picture sometimes good and sometimes evil—and I must not be attached to any picture. I must not gloat over the good, and I must not fear the evil: I must realize the unreal and impersonal nature of both.

The function of the Christ is to break our attachment to "this world," to the pictures of "this world." It acts to overcome our love of the good things of "this world" and our fears and hates of the evil things of "this world" in the realization that both the good and the evil appearances are but appearances, the human dream, if you like. "Awake thou that sleepest."[3] Why are we told that we must awaken? Because as human beings we are asleep, and in that sleep we are in a dream-state, dreaming of both good and of evil.

At no stage of our unfoldment, from the very first day that we undertake the study of the Infinite Way until the last day of our stay on this earth-plane, must we ever permit ourselves to forget these two major principles: (1) the attainment of the consciousness of the presence of God; and (2) all error has its origin in the universal belief in two powers.

When we meditate and do our preparatory work for the day, our protective work, our world work, or our work for our families, we should at least know the goal of that work. We must know what we are going to do when we begin to meditate: we are going to remember consciously that the Spirit of God is closer than breathing, that within our consciousness is the fullness of the Godhead bodily, and that God is fulfilling Himself as our individual experience. God is fulfilling Himself in an individual way, in one as an artist, in another as a merchant, a lawyer, or as a statesman. In any and every form is God fulfilling Himself; God is fulfilling Himself at our particular level of consciousness, at our particular state of receptivity. This must be consciously remembered and then, as we think individually of the members of our families or of our patients or students, again we are remembering: God is fulfilling Himself as the individual experience of this one or of that one, and therefore, he is at the point of fulfillment, at the point of transparency in which, through which, and as which God is appearing on earth.

Then, too, as we deal with the appearances of everyday human living—national conflicts, international conflicts, family conflicts, or individual conflicts—we realize that we are beholding only the activity of a universal belief in two powers. We never will know harmony until we recognize that whatever we are dealing with is but a belief in two powers, and then establish ourselves in the realization:

"I and my Father are one." [4] *In this oneness, the infinite All-power, which is spiritual, is the only Presence and the only Power functioning in my experience.*

It is not that we choose the good over the evil. Rather do we relinquish the good *and* the evil and exchange these for the spiritual. We do not prefer the good to the bad, but we renounce both good and bad, and consciously realize:

Since God constitutes the law of my being, I am governed by spiritual Being, spiritual Law, spiritual Light, and spiritual Truth.

If we engage in this daily practice—and we must—we shall soon find that we have received in our inner being the secret of the universe, the secret of harmony, the secret of the Holy Grail. We shall find that we have the secret of life, once we know that the consciousness of the presence of God is the only reality unto us and that there is no two-law universe. There is only the spiritual-law universe of God. When we have that, the discords and inharmonies will melt gradually, but certainly and completely.

Never Believe That You Know What to Pray For

When we have mastered these two major principles of the Infinite Way, the occasion often arises for us to deal specifically with the problems of the world, and here is another principle. Although these principles should not be divided into major and minor principles, because they are equally important, I still cannot put this additional principle in quite the same category as the first two.

Our attention has been centered so much on the things of this world that even when we are in prayer, we have prayed for specific things. It is certainly abundantly clear that the world has not advanced much in the thousands of years it has engaged in this kind of prayer; it has not overcome the discords of the world in that way, and therefore, in our work, we have found it more efficacious not to pray for anything, but to pray for the attainment of the realization of God, and stop there. When the realization of God is attained or felt, those things necessary to our experience have a way of being added unto us.

I can illustrate that for you by pointing out that when I am meditating or praying about this work and am faced with giving a lecture or a class, I never pray to be given a message to deliver. I never ask for a message for today; I never seek a subject for a class. When I meditate, it is only for the realization of God's presence, and then I find that whether seated or standing on the platform, the message comes, and usually a message of such a nature that it meets some specific need.

Think for a moment. Would it make any difference at all what message you found in this chapter, if the presence of God were not in it? Would any message be of any importance to you or could it do anything for you, if the presence of God were not with the message? On the other hand, would it make any difference at all if there were no message, or what form the message took, if the presence of God were consciously with you? The point is that if you had to choose between having the presence of God with you or having an inspiring message, you would undoubtedly choose the presence of God, even if you had to read a dull message, or listen to a message that at the moment meant nothing to you, or one that you did not understand. What difference would that make to you if, in the message, you felt an actual experience of God's presence, something touching your consciousness, giving you a moment of inner freedom or peace?

Can you see that it is not too important what I actually say on the platform? It is really not too important what form the message takes; but it is important, and vitally so, that the presence of God be realized before I go on the platform and that that realization continue during those moments I am there. The message will then do its work, regardless of its nature or form, or regardless of what particular words come forth.

Whether you have an article of merchandise or a service to sell, or whether you have some work of a physical or mental nature to perform, sooner or later, you are going to discover that the work will be perfectly accomplished only if you have attained the conscious awareness of the presence of God. The attainment of that awareness, of that Presence, goes before you to establish the relationships with those whom you need to contact, whether in buying or selling or in any relationship; but if you depend on your human personality, your human sales ability, or on your human talents, somewhere, sometime, you will fail. If you give less concern to what you are going to say, however, and more concern to the attaining of the realization of the Presence, you will find that the right words for the right occasion will come forth from your mouth.

Never be tempted to believe that you know what you should pray for. Never be tempted to believe that you know what is for your good, because, regardless of what you may believe to be your good at the moment, it is a belief stemming only from the limited state of your present awareness. If you could have the divine Grace to see your life in its wholeness and completeness, it would then be revealed to you that what you, at this moment, think is for your ultimate good may not be so. Many have believed that a college education was an absolute necessity, and others have proved that they could be successful without it. Many have thought that their work lay in some particular field of activity, but had they trusted divine Wisdom to guide them, instead of their limited, finite, human wisdom, something entirely different might have unfolded for them. You have no way of knowing what experience is best for you unless you permit yourself to be guided by a Wisdom higher than your own.

When you enter prayer, do not believe that your wisdom is sufficient to tell you what to pray for, or how to pray. Sad is the lot of the person who believes that he knows how to pray, because every prayer is unique. Every prayer or meditation is different from all other prayers and meditations, and heaven help the person who goes into prayer and meditation with a memory of how he prayed or meditated yesterday for he blots out for himself the possibility of receiving fresh manna today. The safest course for an Infinite Way student to follow is to admit freely that he does not know how to pray, how to go out or come in, or what to pray for, and then open himself in receptivity to that still small Voice which is within, closer than breathing, and let It pray through him, let It utter Its voice, let It have Its way. If you are praying for someone else, let It inform you, let It inform your patient or your student.

Do not try to be Omniscience yourself in your praying, because you can be Omniscience only when you are completely absent from the personal sense of self, when you are absent from any knowledge, when you have attained that place of unknowing in which you definitely know that you do not know, and do not even want to know, but are willing and open to receive spiritual wisdom, spiritual guidance, spiritual strength.

When you are praying or meditating for someone else, do not try to transfer thoughts to him, do not try to know what is right for him or best for him, but sit in a state of complete receptivity, and then let the Father function as your consciousness. You may not receive any message for your patient or student, but you do not need any. He will receive it, and he will receive it not from you, but from the *Source* of you. Your consciousness acts only as the instrument of contact, and you yourself may never know what the message is, or even whether any message has been received. In my practice, it is never given to me to know what message my students or patients receive, and furthermore, I never concern myself with this phase of the work. Many times when they ask if I have received anything for them, my answer is, "No, I have received nothing for you. I have merely meditated, and whatever is to be known or experienced must come to you from the Father. I do not enter the picture of your life except as a transparency, nothing more, nothing less."

Whatever it is that you may feel as the result of Infinite Way prayer or treatment work, or in our meetings, or in any work that is done for you—whatever you feel, you are feeling from the Source Itself for nothing is being directed to you. I do not concern myself with your problems, nor with the solution to your problem because the only solution that I know is the actual realization of God's presence, and the understanding that this problem, whatever its name or nature, is a state of universal hypnotism, without a person through, as, or upon whom it can act, and without a law or a power to create, maintain, or sustain it.

I would emphatically caution every Infinite Way student never to lose these basic points and never to try to advance beyond them, because whatever measure of harmony is to come into our experience through the message of the Infinite Way must come through the understanding and practice of these major principles. As we go further into the mystical side of the message of the Infinite Way, we come into an ultimate awareness and the actual experience of our true identity, but this never, never eliminates the necessity for practicing these basic points.

The Practice of the Principles Is an Aid to Meditation

Those who experience difficulty in meditation are undoubtedly neglecting one or more of three basic principles: (1) the attainment of the consciousness of the presence of God, (2) all error originates in the belief in two powers, (3) never pray for any thing—or they may be attempting to meditate without first having some minutes of contemplative meditation to prepare consciousness for the final moments of listening. In contemplative meditation, we contemplate the presence of God, the unreal nature of the appearance, and the truth that we are not seeking anything in this world, any condition, or any person, but only the realization of divine Presence and Power, the Spirit Itself.

After this contemplative meditation, we can settle down into the experience of meditation: into an inner stillness, an inner peace, an inner calm, which comes as the result of this contemplative meditation and really prepares our consciousness to be still. Through our contemplative meditation, we deal with the problems that may be disturbing us, and therefore in our meditation we are no longer faced with problems, but with the remembrance of what we have been realizing and are then able to take the attitude:

"Speak, Lord; for thy servant heareth." [5] *I am prepared to be still and hear Thy voice. I am inwardly prepared, in quietness and in confidence, to receive Thy grace.*

Those who have difficulty with meditation should give more time to the contemplative form of meditation and practice these three basic principles until they actually experience a release, and then they can settle down into an inner listening attitude and receive God's grace. God's grace is not something we need to earn or deserve; God's grace is not going to be withheld because of some sin of omission or commission; God's grace is not going to be withheld for any reason, for God is not a withholding God. Regardless of your past sins or present sins of omission or commission, God's grace will be experienced if you can open yourself wholeheartedly to receive the Presence and the Grace.

Grace will be given to you. It was given to the woman taken in adultery when she asked for it; it was given to the thief on the Cross: not after years of torture, penalty, and punishment, but in a moment of Christhood. Even if there exists in you the potentiality of sin and disease, remember that these, too, will be taken from you by this grace of God that you receive.

Across the Desk

For those of us on the spiritual path, it is necessary to know beyond all question of doubt the nature of spiritual power. Never forget that there are no human answers to the problems of the world today. No one in Washington, London, Paris, Bonn, or Moscow is going to come up with a solution to the world's troubles. The situation is beyond human power.

The hope of the world must be in spiritual power and those who have gained some measure of understanding of the nature of spiritual power must remain awake in this hour to give the world the benefit of that understanding. It will change your concept of God and pave the way for God-realization to ponder this from the chapter "God Is One" in *Living the Infinite Way*.[6]

According to the Master's teaching and the teaching of all spiritual wisdom throughout the ages, there is only *one* power, *one* law, and *one* being. Think, now, because this is the point to which we are leading: There is nothing in all this world to use God-power for or against. . . . There is not good or strong power, not good or evil power: There is only power—*God is*. There is no power to oppose anything, so there is no use praying to it to overcome our enemies . . . since there is only one power and the power that is, *is* God.

Do you now begin to perceive the nature of spiritual power? Do you understand how to face the threats emanating from temporal power, the "arm of flesh"? Do you perceive the nature of your responsibility to the world since you are of the few who understand the nature of spiritual power? Rise, Students, in the full stature of your understanding to "rest in His word," to "put up thy sword," and know why!

~ 10 ~

MEDITATION ON LIFE BY GRACE

The greatest spiritual blessings that come into your experience are not brought about so much by what you know of truth as by the degree of silence you can maintain. What you know of truth, that is, of the letter of truth, acts only as a foundation for the real demonstration of spiritual living.

Beyond a few simple statements of truth which every truth student must understand and realize, there is little of an intricate or difficult nature that one has to know so far as knowing truth is concerned. The difficult part comes in developing a state of consciousness which enables him to be inwardly still.

Except for the realization of the true nature of prayer, which carries with it the understanding that God does not have to be appealed to or used, and the understanding that all the presence, substance, power, and law of God are where you are, silence is far more valuable than all the speech and all the teaching that can be given. That is why a person can usually do far greater work as a practitioner than as a teacher because a teacher is constantly being called upon to speak, and what he says sometimes deflects from the inward realization that God is. To be able to abide in the is-ness of God is far better than all the teaching or talking in the world. It is not what a person says that does the greater works: it is the quiet, peaceful realization.

The first and very simple rule is not to reach out to God for something, to be sure that you do not believe you need a God-power, and to realize constantly that your only need is for the realization of God's grace. Aside from that, the less talking you do about what you know the better for you and for those you are helping.

This is especially true for those who are teachers because it is when they are not teaching that they are living closest to their spiritual center. Then, they are not thinking and speaking through the mind, saying things that oftentimes sound foolish. Words always sound foolish to the real teacher because anyone who has advanced to the point of being a teacher knows that God is not reached through speech or through thought: God is reached only through silence. The one legitimate excuse there is for voicing truth is to teach it, and the only reason for remembering even a little bit of truth is so that you can settle down in conscious union with God and thereby in union with your good.

God's Omnipresence

Most persons believe that there is a power of good and a power of evil, and they are always trying to get some power of good to do something to a power of evil. As you enter the spiritual life, however, you soon become aware of the fact that all mystical teachings, and especially the revelations of Christ Jesus, are based on the concept or idea of "resist not evil," and "take no thought."

The major point that everyone on the spiritual path must constantly remember is that he is not seeking a power—not even a God-power—to do anything for him or for anyone else. It is not that he does not need God-power, because God-power is forever present; but no one can bring the power of God into his experience by praying for it, by asking for it, by sacrificing, by being good, or by observing rites, rituals, fast or feast days.

God is omnipresence. "The place whereon thou standest is holy ground"[1] because the presence of God is there. So you do not have to spend time wondering how to reach God, how to bring Him into your experience, or how to make yourself worthy of Him, but you live and move and have your being in the realization that wherever you are, God is. It makes no difference whether you are sick, momentarily sinning, temporarily in lack or limitation, or even if you are dying. Right where you are, God is, and your function is merely to keep remembering that, but not to try to make it happen because it is already true.

Never forget that you do not have to ask God for anything: God is already closer to you than breathing; God is already omnipresent where you are; and more than this, God is the all-knowing intelligence that already knows your need. Therefore, do not waste any time telling God what you need or when you need it or how much you need because it is His good pleasure to give you the Kingdom.

Why We Do Not Experience the Kingdom

The question may arise in your mind: If God is present, if God already knows my need, if it is God's good pleasure to give me the Kingdom, then why am I not experiencing it? The only answer to that question is that instead of recognizing that God is, that God is present where you are, that God already knows your need, and that it is His good pleasure to give you the Kingdom, you have perhaps gone way off somewhere trying to find God, trying to get God-power, trying to discover what you can do to bring God into your experience. You have been looking in the wrong direction: You have been looking where God is not, that is, where God is not as far as your immediate demonstration of harmony is concerned.

Moreover, you are perhaps expecting God to give you health, supply, companionship, or home; and if you are, you are praying amiss. The Master is very clear on that point: "Take no thought for your life, what ye shall eat, or what ye shall drink; nor yet for your body, what ye shall put on.[2] . . . If ye abide in me, and my words abide in you, ye shall ask what ye will, and it shall be done unto you."[3] Abide in what words? The word that God is and that God is where you are, that God does know your need and gives it to you freely, and that your function is to relax and to be a beholder, letting God's grace unfold.

Being infinite, God cannot give you anything but Himself, and when you pray for something other than God, you are praying amiss. When you pray to God for health, for peace on earth, for supply, for home, or for companionship, you are praying like the pagans who began this whole practice of that kind of petitionary prayer thousands of years ago.

There is only one legitimate thing for which to pray to God and that is for the realization of God's presence and God's power. It is legitimate to ask God to give you Himself, but nothing else. As a matter of fact, there is nothing else anyone could need or want. When you have attained the realization of God's Self, you will recognize how wise and true was the Master's statement, "All these things shall be added unto you"[4]; only be sure that you are not taking thought for these things, and that your whole desire is for the understanding of God:

Where I am, God is; and God knows all about me. He knows my need before I do, and it is His good pleasure to give me the Kingdom. I will relax and rest in His word; I will not seek to use a God-power, nor will I seek to influence God.

As you go through the day, discords will most likely present themselves to you, and oftentimes they will be in the form of erroneous persons. If so, you will be called upon to realize that in the presence of God there is only the person of God's creating. At other times, evil may present itself to you as some kind of a negative law: a law of matter, weather, or climate, and it will be necessary for you to know that inasmuch as God is Spirit and infinite, the only law must be spiritual law.

When your prayer is a complete relaxing in the Word, you are fulfilling the requirements of prayer, the prayer which is a realization of God's presence and power.

God Is Your Dwelling Place

Many persons have been taught that if they wanted something, they should pray for it. If they needed a new home, they prayed specifically for a new home or did "mental work" about it. But in the Infinite Way, or for that matter in any other mystical teaching, no one would do "mental work," take thought, or pray about attaining or acquiring a home. What he would do would be to settle down into a meditation, and if he found it difficult to become still, he might begin by realizing:

There can be only one home because I live and dwell in God; I live and move and have my being in God.

Who would want to live in any other place? Who would want any other home? Heaven forbid that I should want any home other than the "secret place of the most High," or that I should ever desire to be any place other than "hid with Christ in God," established in my spiritual home in the bosom of the Father.

"He that dwelleth in the secret place of the most High"[5] will always have a beautiful home. And so, as you ponder this idea of your real abiding place for just a few minutes, you become very still. Now you have no desires; now you are not struggling to get something; and when you have released your desire for anything in this world, you automatically find yourself at peace. Then, in quietness and in stillness, there comes this conviction:

Where God is, I am. I am ever in His presence because I and the Father are one, and all that the Father has is mine.

That will constitute your prayer or meditation, and then having attained the realization of your oneness with God, what you call your physical dwelling place, your house or human home, will appear. You will not have to chase after it. It will chase you. You will not have to hunt for it: It will run around hunting for you until it finds you.

Dealing with Daily Problems

If your problem were one of finding employment for yourself or a member of your family, the one thing you would never do is to pray or do "mental work" for employment. Again you would turn to the Father within:

God is infinite, and therefore God must be the only employer; but since God is infinite, God must also be the only employee. Employer and employee are not two beings separate and apart from one another. God is both employer and employee, one and not two, inseparable and indivisible.

The Father says, "Son . . . all that I have is thine,"[6] *so whatever employment the Father has, the son has. And this is not in the future tense: This is in the present tense—now. All that the Father has is mine—all the activity, all the employment, all the recognition, all the reward.*

All that the Father has is mine, for "I and my Father are one."[7] *We are not two; we are not separate from one another; we are not divisible: we are indivisible; we are one: and so employer and employee are one.*

Here where I am, I and the Father are one, and in this oneness is my completeness.

Just as you do not have to chase after a house, so you will not have to chase after employment. Employment will chase after you because it is already a part of your oneness with God. Since in your oneness with God you are inseparable from God, you are also inseparable from your good—from your dwelling place, from your employment, from your supply.

God is my supply: God is my meat, my wine, my bread, and my water. God is all these things. When God gives me Himself,

He is giving me bread, meat, wine, and water. God's selfhood is my food, my clothing, my habitation, and my transportation.

In other words, when you have the conscious realization of your oneness with God, you have supply. To pray for supply, do "mental work" for supply, or seek God's power to get supply would actually act as a barrier to the demonstration of your supply. The only demonstration of supply you can make is the demonstration of conscious oneness with God.

How can you pray for health when God is the health of your countenance? God has no health to give: God is Himself health, and when you have God you have health. Any prayer for health or any "mental work" for health is a waste of time because the only real demonstration of permanent health is the attainment or achievement of God.

Only One Legitimate Desire

Inasmuch as God already *is* and is closer than breathing, you cannot really achieve God: you can only achieve the realization of God's presence, which is already always with you. When you stop trying to get health and understand that there is but one thing to get and that is a realization of God, you become quiet, and something marvelous happens inwardly and outwardly when you stop desiring something external to yourself.

I seek nothing outside of me: nothing and nobody. I have no desire for anything in this world, except to know Thee "whom to know aright is life eternal."

I can give up all other desires because in knowing Thee aright, I am at one with my entire demonstration of life, harmony, wholeness, completeness, and perfection.

Let me say to you now, to you, my students, that after all the work that has been going on with you these many months and years, you have been brought to this place of realization where you should now have the capacity to drop all worldly desires. All that has taken place these past months and years has lifted you into a consciousness where you should now have the capacity inwardly to close your eyes in this conviction:

The whole kingdom of God is within me. I do not have to look outside to "man, whose breath is in his nostrils"[8]: I do not have to look outside to "princes": to person, place, thing, circumstance, or condition. I do not have to go to holy mountains or holy temples or even to holy books.

All that I need now and all that I shall ever need is already within me. All that I could ever hope to achieve by prayer, by study, and by meditation—all this—is now within me, and I need not look outside. I need not attempt to demonstrate anything; I need not attempt to pray. Now I can commune with God within, releasing myself from all desire for any earthly thing.

You can always know whether or not you are praying aright. Do you have in mind the attainment or accomplishment of any earthly thing? If so, you are not praying aright. Each one may use this as a yardstick: "What am I desiring? What is the object of my prayer?" If it is any earthly thing, if it is anything in the external realm, you are praying amiss. But when you are praying and knowing that your desire is to know Him aright, to realize His grace, when your desire is to abide forever in the "secret place of the most High" that you may know His will, then you are praying aright.

"Let the words of my mouth, and the meditation of my heart, be acceptable in thy sight." [9] *Let the meditation of my heart be a continuous song of praise and joy. The kingdom of God is within me. How I love Thy laws—Thy spiritual laws! How love I Thy grace! How I love to tabernacle with Thee—to live and move and have my being in an inner realization that Thou art ever with me.*

"Yea, though I walk through the valley of the shadow of death, I will fear no evil: for thou art with me." [10] *Thou leadest me beside the still waters; Thou makest me to lie down in green pastures. Oh, that my life might be lived in Thee, for Thee, and with Thee, and that I may always be satisfied with Thy great gift of Grace.*

"The earth is the Lord's, and the fulness thereof," [11] *and "Son, thou art ever with me, and all that I have is thine."* [12] *How can I then desire anything from anyone? How can I desire any condition or any circumstance? I can only abide in the center of my being and realize with gratitude that in quietness and in confidence is my peace: not in taking thought, not in seeking a God-power, but in quietness and in confidence do I find my peace, my rest, my abundance, my companionship, and my home.*

Only when I have God does my human companionship appear and appear harmoniously; only when I have God do I have abundant supply; only when I have God do I have health.

God is within you now, and you are in God now; you already have God's presence where you are; but it is your conscious remembrance of that Presence which brings it into manifestation.

"Seek ye first the kingdom of God, and his righteousness; and all these things shall be added unto you"[13]— only be sure that you are not seeking things. Train yourself to have no desires, but the one great desire to know God:

I have no desire but the desire to walk with God, to serve God, and to love God. I have no desire but that God's grace may be revealed to me, that God's law may be made known to me, and that God's will may be expressed in me. All my desires, all my longings—all these have to do with God, not with anything or anybody external to me.

I already have the kingdom of God within me. What more can I have? As I abide in that Kingdom and am still, the feeling of God's presence comes alive in me; there is an awareness that I am one with God and that God is on the field. There is nothing more to do: just to be quiet and let my heart overflow with gratitude.

Your Own Will Come to You

The enlightened consciousness that is attained is itself the health and the bread and the meat and the wine. It is not that you gain enlightenment and then do something with it, but when you receive enlightenment you have nothing further to do, for *it* is doing and being. You are but the beholder of what this light is doing.

The light is attained in that moment when you have no external desires, when you have the knowledge that it is only God's grace, God's will, and God's law that you are desiring to know. It works like a charm. The moment you stop chasing something, it begins chasing you; the moment you stop desiring something, it comes into your experience; the very moment you stop running after something, it begins running after you. As your desire for anything, anybody, or any condition in the external world comes to an end, you begin to live this inner life of conscious oneness with God, and then your external life begins to take care of itself. There is an invisible Presence, Something that you cannot see, hear, taste, touch, or smell, going before you to make the crooked places straight, to prepare mansions for you, and to bring unto you your own. It is very much like what Burroughs says in his poem "Waiting":

> Serene, I fold my hands and wait,
> Nor care for wind, or tide, or sea:
> I rave no more 'gainst Time or Fate,
> For, lo! my own shall come to me.

When you no longer want that which is external and which you believe is for your good and when you are willing to let God fulfill Himself as you and abide only in the desire for spiritual realization, you will find that your own will come to you, too: your dwelling place, your transportation, your food, your clothing, your housing, your employment, your investments. Whatever is of a rightful nature that should be a part of your human experience comes to you because it is a law that the Word becomes flesh, becomes experience, form, and effect, not by virtue of what you may do, but merely by virtue of your inner life of contemplation and realization, a life of living, moving, and having your being in God and having God live and move and have His being in you, so that God and you are eternally one in realization.

Actually, you are already one in relationship, but without the conscious awareness of that oneness, it is as if there were no God in your experience.

Conscious awareness, conscious knowledge, conscious realization: always remember those important words. You must be conscious of something before it can be manifested in your life. Therefore, if you want God and God's grace in your life, you must constantly be consciously aware of God's presence.

Undoubtedly, there are people in the world whose only desire is for money, name, and fame, and if they are willing to struggle and devote their twelve, fourteen, or sixteen hours a day to the attainment of those things, they will most likely gain them. But how many who have succeeded have found after they have attained that success that it was dust in their hands and that it brought no satisfaction, peace, or comfort—sometimes not even safety or security?

On the other hand, those who spend only a few hours of the day consciously aware of an indwelling Presence, of God as the Substance of their good and as the Source of peace, safety, and security, find that God is their high tower and fortress. God cannot give safety and security; God can give only Himself, but in God there is safety and security. God cannot give peace to anyone: God can give only Himself, but in God there is peace.

Seek Me

"In thy presence is fulness of joy.[14] . . . Where the Spirit of the Lord is, there is liberty."[15] Do you not see that the world has lost its way *seeking* peace, safety, security, home, supply, and companionship when all the time the great need was to seek God, seek the realization of God's presence, seek to know Him aright. Turn within again and again and realize:

The kingdom of God is established within me. I do not have to go anywhere or seek anything. I need only know: be still and know. "Be still, and know that I am God." [16] *Be still and know that I who am speaking to you from within am He. Be at peace; fear not. I am He and I am with you; I was with you before Abraham was; I will be with you unto the end of the world. Why seek anything? Why desire anything? Why pray for anything? I am here in the midst of you, and I will give you all things: more than you yourself could ever ask for or know or want. But leave it with Me.*

I *am here in the midst of you. Trust Me; listen for My voice. Be still and know that I, here in the midst of you, am God. Be still and know that I am closer to you than breathing–I, God, am closer to you than breathing. You need not fight; you need not struggle. It is not by might, nor by power, but by My Spirit, by the I that is within you. Relax, sit back, be quiet.*

In quietness and in confidence, everything will be revealed to you. In My presence, there is fulfillment. Where My presence is, there is peace, there is safety and security and harmony.

My *grace is functioning within you–the grace of God. Rely on It. "My grace is sufficient for thee."* [17] *Rest, abide in this Word, and let this Word abide in you.*

"I will never leave thee, nor forsake thee." [18] *Relax. I will be with you unto the end of the world. Do not struggle; do not strive. I in you, and you in Me! What else is there? What more is there?*

I *am your bread, meat, wine, and water. I am the resurrection of your body–I, this Power within you, is the resurrection.*

It will rebuild your body if the years of the locusts have eaten it. "Destroy this temple, and in three days I will raise it up" [19] *—I, in the midst of you, not somebody up in a holy mountain or somebody in a holy temple. No, I in the midst of you will raise up the temple of your body, a whole new body, if you will just relax in* Me, *relax in the assurance that I have been with you since before Abraham was and that I will never leave you, nor forsake you.*

I am the resurrection of your body, the resurrection of your home, the resurrection of your fortune and of your fame. I am the resurrection of anything you have ever lost. I am the resurrection and I am the life, and this I that I am is the I that is within you, closer to you than breathing and nearer than hands and feet.

But do not seek Me *for loaves and fishes: seek* Me *for* Me; *seek to abide in* Me; *seek to know* Me *aright—*Me *in the midst of you. Seek to find your peace and safety and security within* Me. *Do not seek loaves and fishes: seek the realization of* Me, *and I will be the Presence that goes out before you to make the crooked places straight. I will be the love that greets you in every Soul.*

Self-Surrender

Now, in a completely relaxed meditation, give up this world, give up all desire. You have the capacity now to give up all desires except the desire to know God aright, to drop the concern for health, supply, or home, to drop all anxiety for friends or relatives. Drop it all into God because if God cannot take care of it, you certainly cannot; but God can, if you are willing to surrender your concerns and your desires.

Remember, you cannot hold on to something *and* surrender it. You cannot surrender anything *and* hold on to it. Either you are going to hold on to it and learn ultimately that you of yourself could not do it, or you are going to surrender it. Surrender all anxiety for yourself or for anyone else. Surrender all concern for yourself or for anyone else:

I surrender all things unto Thee: I am not withholding anything; I am keeping no mental images in my mind to be concerned about. My only desire is to know Thee aright, to live forever in the remembrance that Thou art in me, and that Thy whole kingdom is within me. I rest in Thy grace; I rest in Thy peace.

Father, forgive me, if I have sought anything but Thy peace and the health of Thy countenance. Father, forgive me if I have ever sought anything but Thy grace or felt that I ever needed anything but Thy grace. Thy grace is my sufficiency. I live by Thy grace; I live because I am an heir of God and joint heir with Christ.

Earthly woes, earthly concerns, earthly anxieties—all these drop away because I am home in Thee, one with Thee. Thou art in me, and I in Thee, and therefore we are one. In that oneness is my completeness, my wholeness, my perfection. If I had Thee and the whole world, I would have nothing more than if I had Thee alone.

I dwell constantly in the realization that where Thou art I am, that we are inseparable, indivisible, and that Thou knowest my need. It is Thy good pleasure to give me the Kingdom—the Kingdom that is already established within me.

Thou wilt never leave me, nor forsake me. If I am good or bad, rich or poor, sick or well, Thou wilt never forsake me. Through the realization of that, the lost years of the locust are restored, and I am whole again: whole through the realization of Thy presence, through the realization of inseparability and indivisibility. God is the Father and God is the Son, and we are one. In this conscious oneness is my Allness.

The sun, the moon, and the stars up there in the sky are all under God's government; the tide is coming in and going out under God's government; trees, grass, and plants are growing; flowers are blooming; fruit is ripening—all under God's grace. The cattle are grazing on a thousand hills under God's grace. Coal and diamonds are in the ground, and pearls in the sea, all under God's grace. Substances that we are using from the ground today were placed there thousands of years ago; substances that will be needed thousands of years from now are forming in the earth and in the water now.

Every need is provided for by God's grace. God's grace is indeed my sufficiency. All things have been given to me by God's grace: not by might, not by power, not by prayer, but by God's grace. So I relax into God and receive the same God-government that directs the earth and all its activities. I am in Thee, and Thou art in me—and we are one.

Take no anxious thought for anything in the external realm; take no anxious thought for anyone in the world. The kingdom of God is established within you, and God's grace is your sufficiency. Take no thought!

Across the Desk

One of the greatest discoveries of this age is that our problems are caused by a universal, impersonal malpractice, brought about by the acceptance of the belief in two powers. We can begin to lessen the activity of this malpractice and thereby lessen our problems through the *daily* realization of the impotence of universal belief and the *daily* remembrance that Spirit, or Truth, is the only power operating as individual consciousness.

consciousness.

Our students dare not forget for a single day that whatever transpires in their experience comes as an activity of their own consciousness, and therefore it is essential that there be a constant reminder of God as the one and only Power, the conviction that power is not in person or effect, but *only* in the invisible consciousness of the individual.

Because of mesmeric world sense, we must regularly bring to conscious awareness the understanding of these revealed principles. By a neglect of these principles, we unknowingly accept the problems of human existence. On the other hand, by a conscious remembrance that God is the only power and that there is no power in effect, we dispel the illusory belief in two powers and its activity.

In order to build a consciousness of truth, all Infinite Way students should know the following passages as well as they know their own names:

"The New Horizon," *The Infinite* Way[20]
"God Is One," *Living the Infinite* Way[21]
"Protection," *The 1955 Infinite Way Letters*[22]
"Break the Fetters That Bind You," *The 1958 Infinite Way Letters*[23]
"Contemplation Develops the Beholder," *The Contemplative Life*[24]
"Introduction" and "Love Thy Neighbor," *Practicing the Presence*[25]
"The Relationship of Oneness," *The Art of Spiritual Healing*[26]

~ 11 ~

SUPPLY AND SECRECY

The promise, "Son, thou art ever with me, and all that I have is thine,"[1] implies that it is natural and normal to experience abundance, but unless the principle underlying that promise is understood, supply becomes more or less accidental rather than the manifestation of a definite spiritual principle. Because of an ingrained belief that supply is something that comes to us, many people have devoted a great deal of time to praying for it, time which has been largely wasted because supply does not come to us: Supply finds its way out from within us; supply is something that we express.

Supply is just as spiritual as integrity, loyalty, morality, and honesty, but we cannot pray for these qualities because they are embodied in our consciousness whether or not we are expressing them to the fullest of our understanding. No one doubts but that he possesses a full measure of integrity, honesty, loyalty, fidelity, and benevolence. The question is to what extent does he wish to express these or what excuses can he make for leaving them unexpressed within himself.

Supply is just as spiritual as these qualities and, therefore, to experience supply, it has to be expressed by us. It is not something that comes to us: it is something that goes out from us and then returns. The bread that we cast upon the waters is the only bread that comes back to us. The reason there are so many people with burnt fingers is because they have been trying to get the bread that somebody else has placed on the waters. Life does not permit us to take from another what belongs to him, and therefore, the only supply to which we have spiritual title is the bread that we ourselves place on the waters of life. What goes out from us is what comes back to us, pressed down and running over, but it cannot come back to us unless we first send it forth.

Inasmuch as supply is spiritual, it must be expressed spiritually in order for it to return to us. There are many examples given by the Master as to how we may cast our bread upon the waters. To begin with, he tells us to forgive seventy times seven, to forgive those who in any wise have offended us. He tells us to pray for our enemies and for those who despitefully use and persecute us. This does not necessarily mean those who offend only you or me. If they offend our neighbor, they are offending us; if they offend our country, they are offending us; if they offend our race, they are offending us; and in the last analysis, if they offend this world in any way at all, they are offending us, for we are all parts of one whole. There is only one God, one Father of us all, and we are all brothers and sisters, and for that reason, whoever offends one of us offends all of us.

So it is, then, that under this law of Christ we are called upon to forgive those who offend, to pray for those who persecute and abuse us, and to pray for our enemies even more than for our friends. "For if ye love them which love you, what reward have ye? do not even the publicans the same? . . . Pray for them which despitefully use you, and persecute you; That ye may be the children of your Father which is in heaven."[2] To be the child of God means to be an heir of God, joint heir to all the supply there is in heaven, but we can only become an heir to the riches that God has to bestow as we learn to pray for all enemies, our own as well as those of mankind, as we learn to forgive those who offend us even up to four hundred ninety times. Would we ever have to forgive the four hundred ninety-first time if we had forgiven four hundred ninety times?

Praying for our enemies and forgiving them are two ways in which we can cast our bread upon the waters, two ways, therefore, in which we demonstrate our spiritual supply. Another way of casting our bread upon the waters is to make whatever provision must be made for the orphaned, the poor, and the aged—this in order to prove we love our neighbor as ourselves, and not only the neighbor who is of our own personal or religious household. Our neighbors are the people of every religion, all races and creeds; and therefore, from our tithe, we must make some provision for all of them.

Gratitude as an Evidence of Receptivity

There are many other ways of casting our bread upon the waters, but the greatest of them all is gratitude. Gratitude takes many forms. As a rule, for example, it is a sense of gratitude that prompts the sending of checks to CARE, to foundations for research in tuberculosis, cancer, or to some other favorite charity.

There was a time when gratitude was expressed through the act of tithing, and it was taught that by tithing a person expressed his gratitude to the Source from which he derived his spiritual food and comfort, and that normally meant the church. As long as tithing is done from the sense of gratitude, it is a blessing to those who tithe, and to those who receive the tithes. But when tithing becomes more or less of a bargaining, a barter, or a percentage deal, descending to the point where a person figures that if he gives 10 per cent to God, he will get 90 per cent back, it loses its effectiveness. Care must be exercised that one does not tithe for a reward because if this is done, tithing becomes a business proposition and not a spiritual experience. Today, although tithing is still practiced among the Mormons, the Quakers, and a few other groups, on the whole, it has largely disappeared and is no longer recognized, as it once was, as a means of expressing gratitude for what we receive from the spiritual Source of our lives.

Those who rediscover the joy and privilege of tithing and who adopt the method the Master taught of giving their benevolences anonymously without letting anyone know what they are doing soon learn that there is a Father who seeth in secret and who rewardeth openly.

Gratitude is not thanking God for anything that we have or for anything that comes to us because it is a fallacy to believe in a God who provides only for you or me or sends things exclusively to us. The God we worship is a God who is responsible for all the good on this earth and in all the other planets that exist. In my opinion, gratitude finds its highest expression in the realization of God as the invisible Source of all that is visible. The sunshine, the rain, rivers, lakes, mountains—all these exist as God's expression of His infinite Being, of His infinite abundance spread forth for the sons and daughters of God, not for one or two, not for the favored few, but for all. The fact that so many receive so little has nothing at all to do with God: It has to do with their individual receptivity, and they can only prove the amount of their receptivity by the amount of bread they cast upon the waters.

Gratitude that fish are in the sea and birds in the air, gratitude that there are cattle on a thousand hills, that the trees are blooming and showing forth God's grace in the luxuriance of their foliage, gratitude for all that we witness from waking in the morning until sleeping at night, gratitude for the fact that life continues in sleep as well as when awake, and that even while we are at rest the principle of life is at work for us: the recognition of God as the Source of all these blessings is to me the highest form of gratitude because there is nothing personal in it: it is simply a sense of gratitude that the infinity of God is omnipresent for all to share and that we all share it in proportion to our own receptivity.

There is no favoritism on the part of God: God never gives more to one than to another; God has no favorite children; God has no favorite race; God has no favorite nation. There may have been a time when some of us believed that certain nations were better than others, but the last forty or fifty years should be enough to convince all of us that it is not too wise to claim virtue for one nation as against another. It would be hard to believe that God prospers one nation because it is so good and punishes others with lack because they are so bad.

As we travel the spiritual path, we learn that we do not have health or abundance because of any virtue of our own. When we see good and virtuous men and women suffering from either disease or lack, and on the other hand, rascals by the hundreds abounding in health and supply, it is very difficult to accept the doctrine of a God of reward and punishment.

My many years on this path have demonstrated to my satisfaction that our supply is in direct proportion to our receptivity, that is, to the degree of gratitude that we express in the form of bread placed upon the waters as benevolence, forgiveness, or praying for our enemies because then we are expressing spiritual principles.

There are persons who give away great fortunes, some, it is true, with no ulterior motive, but many who are not giving in accordance with spiritual principles because they are primarily influenced by personal considerations in their giving. It is the motive that is important, not the amount. It is impossible to measure how much anyone should give in order to be on "the right side of God," if the measuring is done in terms of material things. It is not the amount given, but the amount given in proportion to one's immediate possessions that is the important thing. Probably that is why the widow who gave her mite was so greatly blessed. The only measuring stick is how much love is given, how much co-operation, how much recognition, how much forgiving, how much tithing, how much secret praying, and how much secret giving without drawing attention to one's self.

The Seed Must Be Nurtured in Secret

At this point, we come to one of the deepest and one of the least understood principles in all the Master's teaching: the principle of secrecy. In the Sermon on the Mount, Jesus teaches that we are to pray in secret, to let no man know that we are praying, and not to pray to be seen of men. It is important to remember that the Master tells us that those who pray openly do receive some measure of benefit in the eyes of their fellow men, but they lose the benefit that accrues from God; they lose the grace of God. He tells us that we must not do our alms to be seen of men, but secretly, not letting the left hand know what the right hand does. So we have a choice to make: whether to seek the approval of man or the grace of God.

There is a reason for this: Through spiritual teaching, Truth, which is a synonym for God, for love, for the Christ, is planted in us as a seed. If such teaching could be imparted in its fullness at any given moment, it would instantly lift all of us out of ourselves and raise us right up to heaven, but truth-teaching is but the continuous planting of seeds in our consciousness. When it is received in our consciousness, it is not fruit ready to eat, to enjoy, or to share with our neighbor. It is only a seed, and after that seed is planted in our consciousness, it must be cared for, nurtured, fed, and tended. It must be permitted to fulfill itself, take root, break open, and begin to blossom.

It is for that reason that we must keep these gems of truth locked up within us, not sharing them with anybody regardless of how close to us he may be, because if we do, while we may have the approval of those with whom it is shared, we lose the grace of God. A hard saying, yes, but a true one nevertheless, because what we are doing then is giving away what does not yet belong to us and is not yet fruit, but only a seed. This is not too different from caring for a garden. No gardener can plant seeds in his garden and keep digging them up and giving them away and then six months later go back and expect to find a crop. There is nothing there because nature has not been given the chance or opportunity to work; the secret processes that go on deep within the earth have not had their way with those seeds.

And so similarly, a seed of truth planted in your consciousness or mine requires time in which to fulfill itself before it can come into full-blown realization. While it is locked up inside of us in the dark, there is a process going on within us, an invisible spiritual process much like the nine months' period of gestation necessary for the development of the child in its mother's womb. The fetus must remain there for the full length of time; it must be fed; it must be allowed to fulfill itself; and then when its time is come, it can be birthed.

Whether it is our gratitude to God or to one another, whether it is our benevolences, whether it is our forgiving of our enemies or our praying for them—these are seeds of truth that we take within ourselves, that we live with and practice over and over again until one day out pops the babe, and it is a full-blown babe. When our babe of truth is strong, then we can begin to share and give.

That is what our practitioners and teachers are doing. Truth that has come to fruition within them has become a demonstrated truth that they can share, and the fact that it has become demonstrated truth in them makes it of power. Then they are like the Master of whom it was said, "For he taught them as one having authority, and not as the scribes."[3] He spoke with that authority because he had had long, long years—thirty of them—keeping the truth locked up within himself, not trying to preach, not trying to teach, not trying to heal, but just pondering these truths within himself, pondering, thinking about them, living with them, practicing them, and being grateful for them. Then when he was ready, he could go out and demonstrate that which had become full-blown in him—his spiritual Grace.

Very often a truth reveals itself to us when we are reading a book, meditating, or writing. Suddenly a truth that we have known intellectually becomes a living, vital, realized truth, and when that happens we can go out and share it, a giving and sharing with signs following. I have made it a practice never to teach a truth that has not first been realized and demonstrated by me. For many years, students asked me about the Sermon on the Mount, and my answer always was that I had read it but I did not understand it and therefore could not explain it. In 1956, however, a full-grown realization was given to me in the middle of a class while sitting on the platform, and during 1956 this that had revealed itself to me was given out in my classes because now it had become a realized truth. It was not, of course, made public in writing then, but now it has been published as *The Thunder of Silence.*[4]

There are truths in the Bible of which no one has any right to speak except those that come alive in a person, proving and demonstrating themselves in such a manner that one then has something from the Bible to share.

Practice but Do Not Preach

If you can feel any rightness at all in what I have said to you on this subject of supply and begin to practice it, you should remember also to keep it locked up within your consciousness. Find some period each day for forgiving the enemies of the world as well as your own and pray for them. Find some period in each day for tithing of one sort or another; practice setting aside a specific amount of your income for whatever benevolences you wish to support, but keep these philanthropies secret.

Do not talk about the truth you are learning. For example, in this text you have been given three words: Omnipresence, Omnipotence, and Omniscience. Do not talk about these words, because if you do, you will be taking seeds and scattering them on top of the earth instead of burying them in the ground. Rather take those three words into your consciousness, ponder them, and every time that some evidence presents itself to you of an erroneous form of power, realize within yourself that this cannot be true if Omnipotence is true. Every time something presents itself to you of an erroneous or destructive nature, realize within yourself that, in the light of Omnipresence, this presence cannot be. Whenever any temptation comes to you to go to God and tell Him something about your problems, immediately bring to your thought the word Omniscience—all knowledge, all wisdom—and remind yourself that God already knows all.

Work with those three words conscientiously and continuously, but above all things silently and secretly, until they have had time and opportunity to take root in you and come forth as the full-grown babe. Then you will understand the meaning of the Immaculate Conception and the Virgin Birth; you will understand that all conception is spiritual. Ideas of truth are conceived within you. They are like seeds that you plant and work with until they take root within you. Ponder them and rejoice over them until one day you will find these seeds of truth come forth as "virgin birth." Then it will be with signs following, with joy and with singing.

The wise men of the world will come and bow down to that truth that has been born in you; men and women will pay homage to you because of this truth that is now going forth from you into the world to bless it.

It may be that when you first present truth to the world, you too may have to take it down into Egypt and hide it. Always the world's reaction to truth is to attempt to destroy it because truth destroys the comforts of human life, it destroys material good as well as material evil. Truth destroys personal good and raises up in its place divine Love, a Love that we can share with one another, not as members of a small religious group, but a Love that we can share with all our neighbors, whether friends or enemies. We owe our neighbor love regardless of his religious or medical opinions, and we love our neighbor enough even to help finance his hospitals although we may not use them.

Except for those who are searching for truth, truth as a rule makes people very uncomfortable. This is because the more we enter into the Spirit, the further removed we are from the world's modes and means of living. Blasphemy and vulgarities become more obnoxious to us than they were before, and we feel more discomfort over some trifling offense than some persons do over major offenses.

So it is that when truth is presented in a concrete form to those who are still satisfied with this human sense of life, be assured that you are offending them, and they will turn and rend you unless you are wise enough to know that no power has been given to any evil experience. All power is of God and that power is good.

Too often, people want to share the truth they have with others; they see them in distress and feel that what they have could be so important to those they want to help that they try to rush out and tell them about it, but when they are so tempted, they should remember this teaching of secrecy, remember that they may gain a neighbor's good will, but they will also forfeit divine Grace.

Keep truth within yourself until it comes to fruition. Give forth the fruitage of truth, but do not give forth the truth you know. Give forth the fruitage in the form of forgiveness, prayers, tithing. All these things may be done, but keep the secret of it within you until you do know that it is so clearly established in you that you can share it freely and liberally without fear of losing it.

Practice these principles, lock them up within you, ponder them, meditate upon them until they bring forth fruit after their own kind, and then you will really be grateful for this lesson and reap a rich harvest:

> Bring ye all the tithes into the storehouse, that there may be meat in mine house, and prove me now herewith, saith the Lord of hosts, if I will not open you the windows of heaven, and pour you out a blessing, that there shall not be room enough to receive it.[5]

Across the Desk

On my trips around the world, naturally I come into close contact with Infinite Way groups in every country and have the opportunity of seeing, not only the growth of some of these groups and their ever-increasing activity, but also why some groups do not show forth the same increase in numbers or expansion in depth of spiritual attainment. Inasmuch as the same writings and tapes are used by all groups in the Infinite Way, it is obvious that the principal factor in the development of a group is that of leadership.

Our work in the Infinite Way is not an organized work, and there are no schools one can attend. This makes it important for all who have groups to learn thoroughly the letter of the Message and to attain a healing consciousness.

If a student undertakes a group activity before he is well grounded in the letter of the Message or before he has attained some measure of healing consciousness, he naturally will not have the same degree of spiritual unfoldment as those who are further advanced in the letter and the Spirit. These students must, therefore, be very patient and diligent in study and practice until they are adequately prepared, and then they will find that their groups will reflect their own attained consciousness.

Sometimes those who have groups have not yet learned how to instruct others as to what books to study, and how to use the monthly *Letter* in daily experience. Those who attend group meetings naturally look to the person who conducts the meeting to be of help in different ways. They want to know how to study and in what order the books should be read. I have suggested that those new to the message begin with *Living the Infinite Way*[6] so as to gain some knowledge of the basic principles. From there, they should go to a study of *Practicing the Presence.*[7] Once a student begins to be aware of the Presence and to witness the effect of this awareness more and more, there comes an inner quiet that prepares him for a study of *The Art of Meditation.*[8]

When some proficiency in meditation has been attained, the student is prepared for serious study and practice, and is now ready for *The Art of Spiritual Healing,*[9] *The Infinite Way,*[10] *Spiritual Interpretation of Scripture,*[11] and other writings. Young students have the right to expect that those in charge of groups will know which pamphlets should be used for specific help, such as *A Lesson to Sam* and material for young people in *The 1955 Infinite Way Letters,* the booklets *Truth for Professional People* and *Business and Salesmanship* for the businessman or woman, and *The Deep Silence of My Peace* and *The Secret of the Twenty-Third Psalm* for the seeker.

To explain how far the effect of one transformed consciousness can extend, let us take as an example a household of five or six members, an average family of moderate means and reasonably substantial character, with their pleasures and pains, successes and failures, harmonies and discords. One member of this family, seeking for a solution to a problem, wanting to find an inner quiet or peace, or perhaps dissatisfied with the ordinary day-to-day living, learns about a spiritual teaching such as the Infinite Way. One of the first discoveries this seeker makes is that it is not necessary to live like a prodigal, separate and apart from the divine Source of life. Eventually, step by step, he discovers that man does not live by bread alone—by money or amusements—nor does he receive complete satisfaction through human companionships, worldly success, or profits. He soon finds that a oneness with the wellspring of life, the bread or staff of life, is revealed, and the truths learned in study and meditation now form a new and higher consciousness which is the source of a new life: the rebirthed life.

As this higher consciousness evolves through deeper study, practice, and meditation, the student becomes aware of an inner Grace, which now brings new forms of harmony and peace into existence. It not only dissolves qualities characteristic of human nature, disclosing the true spiritual nature, and shows forth a harmony of mind and body which no longer manifests any of the former sins or diseases, but it may also bring to light hidden talents of art, music, literature, or some form of inventive genius. Gradually, the old self with its limitations, fears, and problems begins to fade away as the higher Self evolves, bringing into being the hidden manna of life: the meat the world knows not of.

It quickly becomes apparent to those of sufficient discernment that this transformation is taking place, but, even more than this, it usually follows that this spiritual development of an individual is touching the lives of his immediate household. This may appear as more harmonious human relationships, less of illness, or greater success in the experience of the members of the family.

Thus, in many ways, as an entire family or household is eventually governed and sustained in some measure by the higher consciousness attained by one person in the home, the hold of material sense on every member is lessened, and frequently one or two members of a household, by their spiritual unfoldment, carry the family through many years of health, abundance, and happiness. Furthermore, it is often true that the head of a business, by study, practice, and meditation, becomes a law of peace and success to his entire staff and to all the affairs of the enterprise.

The higher consciousness of one person not only governs his immediate environment, but also has the effect of transforming in some degree the consciousness of all those individuals touched by the newly born person. The evolving spiritual student more often than not becomes the center of a group of seekers or students, and in the degree of his own unfolding spiritual light does he help to raise those who seek him out to higher levels of consciousness, and this naturally is followed by a greater expression of harmony, wholeness, and completeness by those of this group. The attained consciousness of the one draws to itself others and then in turn lifts them.

But now a greater miracle is apparent. As the consciousness of one person unfolds spiritually and becomes a law of good unto the others and thereby helps the others attain their rebirth, now the consciousness of the two or more who are gathered together becomes a law unto a wider circle of homes, businesses, and lives—lives lived less by human emotions and more by divine Wisdom and Love.

Stop now and think of what this means: the attained measure of spiritual consciousness of a dozen to a hundred students becomes the higher consciousness of an entire community and in some measure transforms the lives of all within that larger circle.

Does this not make clear why ten righteous men can save a city and why a few spiritually evolved persons can rule out of their communities the grosser elements of human nature and restore a greater measure of the Father's consciousness on earth as it is in heaven? Do you begin to see how it is that eventually the Garden of Eden will be lived again on earth as consciousness is evolved to a divine state here and there around the world by individuals and small groups who thus become the higher consciousness of these communities?

Watch the effect upon the household and family where one or two become transformed by the Spirit. Observe the classrooms of the teachers who no longer depend purely on human knowledge in teaching, or the effect on the business that has one or more spiritually enlightened souls guiding its affairs. It will not take long to note that in such a neighborhood or community the effect of the undesirable elements lessens, and the wisdom and love in the community become more and more evident.

The secret of life harmonious is first the transformation of the consciousness of an individual which thereupon becomes a light unto his household and gradually a light to the two or more of a group. Then this united spiritual consciousness becomes the higher Self of many households, businesses, and activities, and finally evolves into the divine consciousness of the community, affecting the health, happiness, and even the prosperity of the community, changing the nature of entire neighborhoods, dissolving its fears and animosities, and establishing a spiritual commonwealth.

Such groups active in cities and communities throughout the world will be responsible in time for establishing the spiritual kingdom of heaven on earth because *one illumined consciousness becomes the consciousness of those it touches.*

This is the period in history when the Father's grace is being revealed on earth as it is in heaven. This is the period which is the foundation for all spiritual ages to come. This is the period in which the nature of spiritual power is being revealed to the world. This is the most thrilling period of spiritual discovery ever recorded in history. Those who are part of this revelation of the spiritual age are blessed beyond measure and degree.

No one can know how I rejoice in the spirit that animates our students throughout the world, a spirit which evidences, by its fruitage in so many lives and communities, the consecrated hours they give to God and His children.

Any spiritual message is the grace of God reaching human consciousness, the voice of God being uttered on earth that earthly errors may be dissolved, and certainly this is true of the Infinite Way. It is not my possession, nor yours, except insofar as we are parts of the whole. No one has ever been given an "exclusive" on it. It belongs to all who can receive it, whether of one church or another, or of none.

In several cities at the present time, there are Study Centers where the message of the Infinite Way may be heard or read and where visitors may find spiritual refreshment in prayer and meditation. These are not a part of any central organization, but a service to a community, conducted and maintained by local students and intended only to function as long as they are a service and fulfill a spiritual purpose.

The Study Center will be a spiritual oasis in the human wilderness as long as personal sense is absent from the consciousness of the students who serve and support the activity. They must, however, be watchful of the temptations to come under the spell of self-aggrandizement, ambition, and competition, and be quick to recognize and handle these as universal carnal mind, impersonalizing and "nothingizing" them. The Infinite Way is the gift of God and the possession of no one.

When prosperity comes to a work such as ours, that is the time to be especially watchful. Then, as they did to the Master in the wilderness, temptations come to be something of ourselves and even to believe that we may claim the Christ-message as our own. Be assured that what has been given to me in our work has come from the source and the fountain of Light and Wisdom, and I am but a messenger, "a scribe," writing and speaking "under orders." The principles come from the divine Consciousness to mankind, and all of us who work in this activity are but servants in God's service. Let this never be forgotten by those responsible for the activity of a Study Center, and then the Study Center will fulfill a spiritual function in the community.

Above all, those who serve in this activity must be sure in their own minds that this message is addressed to human consciousness universally: not to one or two segments of it. Since it belongs to those of all denominations as well as to those of none, it must not be organized or set apart as a separate religion, philosophy, or teaching. The name the Infinite Way is a way of designating certain specific revealed principles of spiritual living and healing. It is not something separate from Christianity, Judaism, Vedantism, Hinduism, Taoism, or Zen. Rather must the Infinite Way be seen and understood as a revelation or unfoldment in this age to all who seek spiritual light, communion, and union with God.

As the author of the Infinite Way writings, I have no feeling of ownership or even of authorship. They are copyrighted only for the practical purposes of publication. The royalties and other earnings have carried this message around the world and provided for every personal and family need. They also provide for the present and foreseeable future needs of our work and in other ways contribute to the education and enlightenment of mankind.

~ 12 ~

THE SPIRITUAL CHRISTMAS

In the account of the advent of the Christ in the Gospel according to St. Luke, the Christ was born in a manger because "there was no room for them in the inn."[1] There was no room in the inn, and so the Christ was born in the stable of the inn. Esoterically, the meaning of this is that the human consciousness, which is the place of enjoyment, comfort, and revelry, never has room for the Christ. When there is a sufficiency of supply, health, and the comforts of home life, rarely is there room in that consciousness for the Christ, and because of this human complacency, usually it is only when sickness, sin, or poverty is experienced that consciousness is ready to receive the revelation of the Christ.

More often than not, it is the sick, the sinning, and the poor who are the seekers. Probably in the beginning they seek relief only from their evil, discordant, or unhappy conditions, but sooner or later they awaken to the fact that there is a deeper meaning to the activity of the Christ than merely the healing of the sick or even the raising of the dead. It is then that consciousness is opened to receive the spiritual Impulse.

Within the consciousness of every person in the world, and in the consciousness of all those who have been here and of all those who have not yet come to this plane of existence, there is this spiritual Spark, that which is called the Christ, a Spark which is kindled only as man seeks for It and learns to turn within to find It.

Isaiah Reveals the Christ

In trying to understand the Christ, it is necessary to know Its function and the meaning of the kind of a life that is lived when the Christ is realized. More than any other Hebrew prophet, Isaiah caught the vision of the Christ, and from beginning to end the Book of Isaiah is replete with wisdom concerning the Christ:

Woe to them that go down to Egypt for help; and stay on horses, and trust in chariots, because they are many; and in horsemen, because they are very strong; but they look not unto the Holy One of Israel, neither seek the Lord!

Now the Egyptians are men, and not God; and their horses flesh, and not spirit. When the Lord shall stretch out his hand, both he that helpeth shall fall, and he that is holpen shall fall down, and they all shall fail together.

Turn ye unto him from whom the children of Israel have deeply revolted.

For in that day every man shall cast away his idols of silver, and his idols of gold, which your own hands have made unto you for a sin.[2]

Upon the land of my people shall come up thorns and briers; yea, upon all the houses of joy in the joyous city:

Until the spirit be poured upon us from on high, and the wilderness be a fruitful field, and the fruitful field be counted for a forest.

Then judgment shall dwell in the wilderness, and righteousness remain in the fruitful field.

And the work of righteousness shall be peace; and the effect of righteousness quietness and assurance forever.

And my people shall dwell in a peaceable habitation, and in sure dwellings, and in quiet resting places;[3]

The wilderness and the solitary place shall be glad for them; and the desert shall rejoice, and blossom as the rose.

It shall blossom abundantly, and rejoice even with joy and singing: the glory of Lebanon shall be given unto it, the excellency of Carmel and Sharon, they shall see the glory of the Lord, and the excellency of our God.

Say to them that are of a fearful heart, Be strong, fear not: behold, your God will come with vengeance, even God with a recompense; he will come and save you.

Then the eyes of the blind shall be opened, and the ears of the deaf shall be unstopped.

Then shall the lame man leap as an hart, and the tongue of the dumb sing: for in the wilderness shall waters break out, and streams in the desert.

And the parched ground shall become a pool, and the thirsty land springs of water: in the habitation of dragons, where each lay, shall be grass with reeds and rushes.

And an highway shall be there, and a way, and it shall be called The way of holiness. . . .

No lion shall be there, nor any ravenous beast shall go up thereon, it shall not be found there; but the redeemed shall walk there:

And the ransomed of the Lord shall return, and come to Zion with songs and everlasting joy upon their heads: they shall obtain joy and gladness, and sorrow and sighing shall flee away.[4]

Here in those few verses is recounted the entire function, nature, and purpose of the Christ. In our human state of being, we go down into "Egypt" which symbolizes our going to some place outside ourselves for help: we seek allies, that is, we seek the help of "man, whose breath is in his nostrils."[5] We rely on the horsemen and horses of Egypt; we rely on bombs and bullets; but even more than that, we have fashioned silver and gold until we have come to believe that our salvation and our supply are in them and that our good somehow lies in having an abundance, not necessarily of silver and gold, but of the dollar bills that represent the silver and gold. We have fashioned money and systems of money, and then not only worshiped them, but feared the lack of them as if our salvation were in the currency instead of in the Spirit of the Lord God, which is supposed to be upon us.

We have fashioned combinations of allies and looked upon them, not merely as negotiating instruments, but as if safety and security and peace were actually to be found there or as if they had the power to bestow peace upon the world; whereas it is only the Spirit of the Lord God that can bring peace or endow the organizations man has made with any measure of success.

As long as we look to "man, whose breath is in his nostrils," to his armies, his navies, and his bombs, to combinations of nations and treaties, to gold and silver and to the nation's currency, we are worshiping idols; we are expecting our good to come from form and effect, from the creature rather than from the Creator.

The Christ is an invisible Spirit of God that is within us, awaiting our recognition and acknowledgment. When we look to this Spirit of God within us, we are looking to the Source, the Substance, the Law, and Activity of our good.

Receptivity to the Christ Is Greater in Time of Need

So it is that when we have an abundance of silver and gold, are well supplied with allies, and have archives filled with treaties of one kind or another and depend on these, we are not receptive or responsive to the Christ, that Spirit of God which was planted within each and every one of us in the beginning when we were made in the image and likeness of God, and which is part of our very being.

The consciousness that is preoccupied with its business, its pleasures, and its comforts never has time or place for a receptivity to the Christ. Often it is only when we are depressed, discouraged, and disheartened in spirit, depleted in finances, poor in health, and weak in morals that we finally begin to make room for the Christ. The Christ, therefore, in reality is born in a stable, that is, in the lowest part of our consciousness, and it is there that we have to begin our search, and continue until the tiniest glimpse of spiritual Reality is given to us.

It is at that point that we usually make a mistake. We receive some evidence of the Christ within us, the healing of a physical, mental, moral, or financial condition and, in our enthusiasm, we rush out to impart and show it to the world, oftentimes little realizing that the world at large cares not one whit about it, and cannot even understand or believe it.

Scripture says, "Except ye see signs and wonders, ye will not believe,"[6] and yet the very first time that we are healed of a cold or some other minor ailment, we are so grateful that we are eager to tell about it and so enthusiastic that we almost expect the world to believe it. But Scripture again cautions us to "take the young child and his mother, and flee into Egypt, and be . . . there until I bring thee word"[7]: take the Christ-child down into darkness and hide It from the world. Do not reveal this Christ that has been revealed to you: Do not try to give It to this world; do not try to be a do-gooder; do not try to save the world. The world does not want to be saved any more than you wanted to be saved when you were healthy and prosperous and all was going well.

The world will accept the Christ when the world is sufficiently in need of It: the Hebrews under Pharaoh accepted Moses, but their need was great; the Hebrews under Caesar accepted the Christ, also because their need was great. And so this entire world will accept the Christ when its need becomes great enough. Some evidence of this is becoming apparent because in those countries that have experienced the greatest problems we have found the greatest receptivity and response to this work.

There is within every one of us this Infinite Invisible which, in Christian mysticism, is called the Christ or Spirit of God in man. It is the bread, the meat, the wine, and the water. It is our support and supply. No change takes place in our outer life except in proportion to our awareness of the inner Presence and Power, but as we awaken to this Spirit within us, It becomes the very substance, life, law, and activity of our experience in the without. Therefore, we are not to take thought about the things of the outer world: we are to seek the realization of this inner Presence, and then let our outer world be renewed and resurrected.

The Rejection of the Christ

After this realization that takes place in our consciousness during our periods of sin, disease, lack, or unhappiness—what we may call the birth of the Christ in the stable—we are led step by step through the various activities of the Christ, witnessing how It feeds the hungry, heals the sick, and raises the dead, until we are led to the point of rejection of the Christ, and eventually to the crucifixion. This rejection of the Christ is not a historical event. It is a personal event that takes place in the experience of every individual who has attained even a small measure of the Christ. True, it was an event that took place two thousand years ago, but it also took place four thousand years ago and six thousand years ago and eight thousand years ago, and it has been taking place every year and every day since then.

Unbelievable as it may seem, every spiritual student in the world who has received the Christ has, at some time or other, come to a place of rejecting It. Regardless of what miracles It has performed in a person's life, there still comes a time of temptation, a time of rejection.

Just as this temptation came to the followers of the Christ two thousand years ago, as it has come to every mystic, so will it come today to anyone who remains on the Path because as the Christ begins to operate in our consciousness, It makes our human life somewhat better; It heals our physical diseases; It relieves us of poverty or takes us out of lack and limitation; It begins to improve some of our human relationships; It brings to us a greater sense of companionship. From the human standpoint, it would seem that now we have discovered something like Aladdin's lamp, and all we have to do to make our human experience become better and better and better is to wish and rub on the lamp.

The time comes when the inner realization dawns that the real function of the Christ is not just to make our bodies less painful, our experience more harmonious, or to increase the amount of our income. That is but the kindergarten stage of the Christ-experience. Bit by bit, we begin to learn something of what Jesus meant when he said that his followers must leave all for his sake. Unless we begin to give up faith and trust and hope in the outer world, unless we come to the place of renouncing what the Master called "this world," even a good "this world," we cannot enter the spiritual kingdom. "My kingdom is not of this world,"[8] and even if this world has become a healthy, wealthy, or peaceful one, there is yet another place for us. It is "My kingdom," and it is a world made up of entirely different standards from those of even the very best human standards.

That brings us to that baffling passage in Scripture where Jesus acknowledges that John the Baptist is a holy man: "Among them that are born of women there hath not risen a greater than John the Baptist: notwithstanding he that is least in the kingdom of heaven is greater than he."[9] Here was the greatest, the most righteous Hebrew prophet, and yet the very least of those who had entered the kingdom of heaven were before him!

When we have attained a sense of righteousness and are living under the law, obeying the Ten Commandments, and are beginning to experience healthy and harmonious humanhood, we think we have arrived; but we have not even approached the very least of those who have attained spiritual consciousness. When we are faced with the necessity of relinquishing the idea of merely improving our humanhood, of forgetting for the time being whether we are enjoying good humanhood or wallowing in bad humanhood, of being unconcerned whether momentarily we have or do not have problems, and instead go right to the Center to seek, not what we shall eat or drink, but the kingdom of God and His righteousness, we come to the place of decision; those of us who are unwilling to forsake our human ways turn back to our human holiness, our human health, and our human good, and the Christ is rejected and crucified—gone and forgotten.

Because we attempt to continue demonstrating merely human good we often come to the point of the rejection or crucifixion of the Christ within us, but almost simultaneously with that temptation comes the opportunity to experience the resurrection. This opportunity comes because we realize that now that we have attained health, supply, companionship, and all human good, there remains a void within us, there is a lack, there is something missing. Then it is that the Christ is resurrected within us, raised up from the tomb of forgetfulness or rejection into which we have cast It, and once more It comes alive in us to show us that the ascension lies just ahead.

In this resurrected form, we witness the full activity of the Christ. We see that the Spirit of the Christ within us walks through closed doors and through walls; It is not killed by bullets, bombs, or knives. It is never destroyed, and regardless of the human circumstances that surround us, in three days—at any time—the Christ can raise up our entire experience and lift it into a resurrected form that can produce meat and drink spiritually, that can prove that it is not formed of matter or limited by material conditions and material beliefs, that It is risen above the limitations of human sense, personal sense, and that It has a spiritual life which is Self-maintained and Self-sustained.

True, we are still in this world, but we are not of it any longer. We partake of its good, yet not to the extent we heretofore did, but rather through this resurrected Spirit, which now completely dominates our lives and culminates in the experience described by Paul: "I live; yet not I, but Christ liveth in me."[10] Outwardly, we are flesh and blood and outwardly we perform the same functions in our business, profession, or whatever our work may be, yet it is all taking place because of an inner activity, an inner Spirit by means of which our whole human life flourishes.

Almost everyone who attains the Christ, attains It, first of all, in his most depressed or debased state of mind, and as It proves Itself in his experience and restores unto him the lost years of the locusts and provides him with health and supply, It leads him to that point of realization where he knows that it is not enough for the Spirit of God to give him lodging and three meals a day. He must go deeper and relinquish even the human good, but it is at this point that the Christ is rejected, a rejection usually taking the form of postpone-ment, putting off that day so that the human good can be enjoyed a little bit longer. Oh, yes, he assures himself that he will come to the Christ soon, very soon. He will get into deep meditation and live in and through the Spirit exclusively—not now, but soon.

Then, in the midst of this hesitancy and attempt at postponement comes a period of barrenness in which he may have an abundance of every bit of good that there is on earth, but in spite of all this good there is still an incompleteness, a lack of fulfillment. This period of barrenness is followed by an acceptance of the resurrection in a full and complete willingness to let the Christ lead him into the actual experience of the Christ-life.

The Christ-life on earth is a far different life from merely a happy human way of life. There are different standards to that life, different modes and means of expression. There is no longer a seeking for "me" or "mine," but rather a release from all personal sense.

The Christ Dissolves All Evil

We bring this life to ourselves by living consciously in oneness with God. In the human world, there are ways of acquiring good by our labors, by our planning honestly or conniving dishonestly; but to have all of which we shall ever have need plus the twelve baskets full left over every day is a state arrived at only through spiritual means, through the realization of our conscious oneness with God, of continuously living and moving and having our being in God-realization. But these twelve baskets full left over are not for you or me alone: this abundance is for anyone who opens his consciousness to the realization of Omnipresence. The heavens and the earth and the air and the waters beneath the earth are filled with God's glory, and this for the benefit of all mankind.

To acknowledge the universal nature of God's abundance is to pray for our neighbor. It recognizes our neighbor's right to the same abundance that is on our table, even the neighbor who momentarily may be our enemy. We are praying for our enemy when we realize that God's grace fills this earth and that it is available to all those who no longer place their faith and trust in "horses and chariots," who no longer place their faith in silver and gold, but in the Spirit of the Lord God which is within them.

This spiritual life, this Christ-life on earth, is one in which we no longer think primarily of the blessings of God for us or for our family, or even for the followers of our chosen form of worship, but it is one in which we acknowledge God's grace on earth, one in which we pray that God's good be equally shared by all—at least acknowledging its availability to all.

There is a difference between praying for "my" good and praying for the acceptance of God's good universally and impersonally expressed, a difference which should be followed in every detail of our lives. You remember that when Sapphira and her husband attempted to withhold their possessions from the collective good, Peter reminded them, "Thou hast not lied unto men, but unto God."[11] So, too, whenever we witness injustices or cruelties on this earth, we have the right also to say in our prayers, "You have not done this unto me; you have not done this unto my neighbor or my nation: you have done this unto God," and when we have thus impersonalized it, we have begun to destroy the evil and the injustice.

Impersonalize every error and whatever its nature realize: "This is not happening to the Chinese, the Russians, or the Africans. This is a sin against the Holy Ghost." Any act of injustice, cruelty, or unfairness is not a sin against you or me or mankind: it is a sin against freedom, justice, liberty, equality, which means that it is a sin against God.

You and I should abide in that realization and stop trying to live life from a personal standpoint. "Vengeance is mine; I will repay, saith the Lord."[12] It is not yours or mine. We do not have to seek vengeance on this earth against anybody or any nation. All we have to do is to impersonalize the evil, realizing that "no weapon that is formed against thee shall prosper; and every tongue that shall rise against thee in judgment thou shalt condemn,"[13] because it is not aimed or formed against us. It is formed against the Christ, against our spiritual life and identity. Even if a sword could cut off our human experience, it would not exterminate us. Therefore, it is not really aimed at the human experience: it is aimed at the very Christ, just as the rejection of Jesus by the Hebrews was not a rejection of Jesus, the man, but of the Christ. When he was no longer on earth and there was no human being for the doubter or skeptic to reject, the rejection of the truth that Jesus taught still continued in that day as it does today.

"Though the mills of the gods grind slowly, yet they grind exceeding fine." Every rejection of truth, every evil and injustice eventually come to an end, but their end would have been hastened if the world had been taught these past two thousand years this great and wondrous truth that no weapon that is formed against man shall prosper, because it is not formed against man, but against the Christ, and the Christ is that Spirit which dissolves sin, disease, and all phases and forms of mortality: mortal sense or mortal consciousness.

The Impersonal Christ-Life

The Christ-life is lived in that impersonal way which no longer concerns itself with "my" particular good or yours. We are not concerned merely with using the infinite power of God to make your individual way a little smoother or mine. The Christ-way of life is one that lives by and through a universal Grace and through a realization that what affects one affects all.

Do you realize that when one individual or one group is enslaved, in that degree mankind is enslaved? Do you not know that when one individual or one group is set free, in that degree all mankind is set free? This idea of freedom, which had its beginning with the ancient Greeks but which did not come to fruition until after the

American and French Revolutions, has spread and spread and spread until it has evolved into the idea that the peoples of every nation must become free, independent, and self-governing.

Every one of us can help in the spread of freedom. We can begin even in a small way with grace at our table every day, by recognizing that "the earth is the Lord's, and the fulness thereof,"[14] and that God is saying to everyone on the face of the globe, "Son, thou art ever with me, and all that I have is thine."[15] Grace, when it is rightly understood, is a recognition that only God has placed the crops in the ground, that only God can prosper them, that only God can give us the fruitage of the trees, and that only God fills this universe with good—does not fill you or me, but this entire earth.

From there we are led, step by step, to living the impersonal life, a life that is not seeking merely our own good, our family's or our nation's, but is realizing that what harms one harms all, that what benefits one benefits all, and then we can begin to live in this recognition:

No weapon that is formed against mankind shall prosper, because it is not aimed at mankind, but at the Christ or spiritual Life.

And we let God dissolve Its enemy, that which is antagonistic to Itself, to Its being, Its continuity, Its unfoldment and expression.

We begin with every weapon that is formed against us in our individual life, whether it is a temptation of sin, a temptation of disease, a temptation of lack, or a temptation of loneliness to remember that, on that Holy

Day in which the Christ is born in us, no weapon that is formed against us shall prosper because it is not formed against us, but against God, against the Christ. Then we relax and let this Spirit that is within us dissolve whatever the form of error may be that confronts us. Always our salvation lies in this ability to impersonalize, to live spiritually instead of personally.

The story of the Christ is never completed until the ascension in which we, individually, rise completely above the personal sense of existence and recognize that the activity of God is never to benefit or bless you or me, but that it is a universal activity blessing mankind, and that the weapons that are formed against us are not formed against individual you or me, but against the Christ of being, and then let the Spirit do Its work on earth.

Rejoice that God's grace is upon the earth in the minds and hearts of mankind and that this Grace is now breaking up the pattern of materialism as a preparation for His kingdom, which is being established on earth.

SCRIPTURAL REFERENCES & NOTES

NOTE: The material in *The Contemplative Life* first appeared in the form of letters sent to students of the Infinite Way throughout the world in the hope that they would aid in the revelation and unfoldment of the transcendental consciousness through a deeper understanding of Scripture and the practice of meditation.

Chapter 1
1. Matthew 6:25, 33
2. John 10:30
3. John 10:30
4. *Practicing the Presence,*
   © 1958 by Joel S. Goldsmith (reprinted 1997 by Acropolis Books, Inc., Lakewood, CO).
5. *The Art of Meditation,*
   © 1956 by Joel S. Goldsmith (NY: Harper & Row, 1965, 1990).

Chapter 2
1. John 5:30
2. John 5:31
3. Proverbs 3:6
4. I Samuel 3:9
5. John 5:30
6. Mark 4:39
7. Mark 6:50
8. Hebrews 13:5
9. Mark 6:50
10. Hebrews 13:5
11. ibid.
12. Matthew 28:20
13. John 10:10
14. 2 Corinthians 3:17
15. Psalm 91:10

Chapter 3
1. Matthew 23:9
2. Luke 17:21
3. Galatians 6:7
4. Galatians 6:8
5. Hebrews 13:5
6. Matthew 28:20
7. Psalm 23:2
8. Job 23:14
9. Psalm 138:8
10. Isaiah 30:15

Chapter 4
1. John 13:4, 5, 14
2. Matthew 26:26
3. Psalm 24:1
4. John 18:37
5. John 4:32
6. John 4:13, 14
7. John 5:31
8. Matthew 19:17
9. John 14:10
10. Philippians 4:13
11. Galatians 2:20
12. Psalm 91:1
13. Matthew 7:14
14. Isaiah 26:3
15. Proverbs 3:6
16. John 15:4

Chapter 5

1. 1 John 1:5
2. Zechariah 4:6
3. Isaiah 45:2
4. John 19:11
5. Matthew 5:38
6. Luke 4:8
7. 1 Samuel 17:45
8. Luke 10:17
9. Luke 10:20
10. 1 Samuel 17:47
11. Matthew 6:4
12. Matthew 7:14
13. Luke 17:21
14. Matthew 13:46
15. Matthew 23:37
16. Isaiah 45:2

Chapter 6

1. John 10:30
2. ibid.
3. Psalm 24:1
4. Luke 15:31
5. Psalm 23:4
6. Psalm 16:11
7. John 15:6
8. Romans 8:7
9. John 10:30
10. John 14:28
11. Galatians 2:20
12. Matthew 6:32
13. Luke 12:32
14. Matthew 6:25
15. Isaiah 65:24
16. Luke 12:32
17. Psalm 23:4
18. Matthew 23:9

Chapter 7

1. Galatians 6:8
2. Isaiah 2:22
3. John 19:11
4. Isaiah 2:22
5. Ezekiel 21:27
6. Isaiah 2:22
7. Psalm 23:1
8. *The Thunder of Silence,*
   © 1961 by Joel S. Goldsmith.
9. *The Infinite Way Letters
   1958 by Joel Goldsmith,*
   © 1990 Thelma G. McDonald
   (Marina del Ray, CA, DeVorss
   & Company, 1990).

Chapter 8

1. Matthew 19:17
2. John 8:11
3. John 5:30
4. John 14:10
5. John 18:36
6. Mark 4:39
7. Acts 20:24
8. John 18:36
9. Matthew 14:27
10. Genesis 3:11
11. Ephesians 5:14
12. Psalm 17:15
13. John 10:30
14. Ephesians 5:14
15. Matthew 14:27
16. ibid.
17. John 18:36
18. Matthew 14:27
19. John 18:36
20. Isaiah 2:22

Chapter 9

1. Exodus 3:5
2. John 5:30

224

Chapter 9 (Continued)
3. Ephesians 5:14
4. John 10:30
5. 1 Samuel 3:9
6. *Living the Infinite Way,*
© 1961 by Joel S. Goldsmith
(New York: Harper & Row,
1961; Harper Collins, 1993).

Chapter 10
1. Exodus 3:5
2. Matthew 6:25
3. John 15:7
4. Luke 12:31
5. Psalm 91:1
6. Luke 15:31
7. John 10:30
8. Isaiah 2:22
9. Psalm 19:14
10. Psalm 23:4
11. Psalm 24:1
12. Luke 15:31
13. Matthew 6:33
14. Psalm 16:11
15. 2 Corinthians 3:17
16. Psalm 46:10
17. 2 Corinthians 12:9
18. Hebrews 13:5
19. John 2:19
20. *The Infinite Way,*
© 1947, 1956 by Joel S.
Goldsmith (reprinted 1997 by
Acropolis Books, Inc.,
Lakewood, CO).
21. *Living the Infinite Way,*
© 1961 by Joel S. Goldsmith.
22. *The Infinite Way Letters
1955 by Joel S. Goldsmith,*
© 1992 Thelma G. McDonald
(Marina del Ray, CA, DeVorss
& Company, 1992).

Chapter 10 (Continued)
23. *The Infinite Way Letters
1958 by Joel Goldsmith,*
© 1990 Thelma G. McDonald
(Marina del Ray, CA, DeVorss
& Company, 1990).
24. *The Contemplative Life,*
(See Chapter 8 of this work.)
25. *Practicing the Presence,*
© 1958 by Joel S. Goldsmith.
26. *The Art of Spiritual Healing,*
© 1975 by Emma A. Goldsmith
(Lakewood, CO: Acropolis
Books, Inc., 1997).

Chapter 11
1. Luke 15:31
2. Matthew 5:46, 44, 45
3. Matthew 7:29
4. *The Thunder of Silence,*
© 1961 by Joel S. Goldsmith.
5. Malachi 3:10
6. *Living the Infinite Way,*
© 1961 by Joel S. Goldsmith.
7. *Practicing the Presence,*
© 1958 by Joel S. Goldsmith.
8. *The Art of Meditation,*
©1956 by Joel S. Goldsmith
(New York: Harper & Row,
paperback edition, 1990).
9. *The Art of Spiritual Healing,*
© by Joel S. Goldsmith.
10. *The Infinite Way,*
© 1947, 1956 by Joel S.
Goldsmith.
11. *Spiritual Interpretation of
Scripture,* © 1947 Joel S.
Goldsmith (Marina del Ray,
CA, DeVorss & Company).

Chapter 12
1. Luke 2:7
2. Isaiah 31:1, 3, 6, 7
3. Isaiah 32:13, 15–18
4. Isaiah 35:1, 2, 4–10

Chapter 12 (Continued)
5. Isaiah 2:22
6. John 4:48
7. Matthew 2:13
8. John 18:36
9. Matthew 11:11
10. Galatians 2:20
11. Acts 5:4
12. Romans 12:19
13. Isaiah 54:17
14. Psalm 24:1
15. Luke 15:31